THE FIVE POWERS

Trust
Energy
Mindfulness
Calm
Wisdom

Written by
Stephen Fulder

Illustrated by
Alessandro Sanna

Art Director: **TamarBD**

Editor: **Rohan Saxena** | Consultant Editor: **Kate Adams**

aster

An Hachette UK Company
www.hachette.co.uk

First published in Great Britain in 2020 by Aster,
an imprint of Octopus Publishing Group Ltd
Carmelite House
50 Victoria Embankment
London EC4Y 0DZ
www.octopusbooks.co.uk

ISBN: 978 1 78325 351 7

A CIP catalogue record for this book is available from the
British Library.

Printed and bound in China

10 9 8 7 6 5 4 3 2 1

Production Manager: Caroline Alberti

CONTENTS

Alessandro Sanna

Born in 1975 in Nogara, Italy, Alessandro Sanna today lives in Mantua where he works at his studio in Casa di Rigoletto. Sanna dedicates himself to teaching illustration and drawing in the Fine Arts academies of Bologna and Verona.

He is an author and prolific illustrator of books for children and adults. Considered to be one of Italy's leading contemporary illustrators, he is renowned for his free spirit and unique brushed watercolours technique, allowing the colours to spread as if they had a life of their own.

Sanna's art works are published all over the world, through publishers such as Rizzoli, Einaudi, Emme, MeMo, Corraini, Mondadori and in the magazines *Gioia* and the French edition of *Vanity Fair*. He has also been featured in *The New York Times Book Review* and the *New Yorker*. He has won the Andersen Prize three times.

> *'I believe in things that do not exist,*
> *for this reason I draw them.'* A.S.

Stephen Fulder

Dr Stephen Fulder was born in London in 1946. A graduate of Oxford University, he has a PhD in molecular biology and is an expert in herbal and complementary medicine, on which he has published fourteen books.

Involved in dharma practice since 1975, Fulder has spent years in India and has been guided by a variety of teachers from India, Burma and the West. Fulder has been teaching mindful meditation for a quarter of a century and leads countless retreats, courses and classes, especially for advanced practitioners around the world.

Stephen Fulder is the founder and senior teacher of Tovana, the largest Israeli insight meditation society, making Mindfulness, Vipassana meditation and dharma teachings widely available.

Introduction

It can all feel a bit too much.
We find ourselves occupied, from morning till night -
reacting, responding and coping with uncontrollable and
often difficult circumstances.

Life can seem an endless Sisyphean struggle, as we push the rock uphill only to watch it roll down once again. How can we rise above challenges such as stress, anxiety, depression, frustration and the myriad of other conflicts and unhappiness that can assail us, meeting them from a place of greater equanimity and expansion? How do we perform a restart? Is it possible to radically transform our daily life? How do we emerge from this sense of endless struggle? How can we invite deeper meaning and more ease, steadiness and freedom into our lives?

There is a Zen story: a seeker wandered far and wide in search of liberation. After many arduous travails, he learnt of an enlightened master that might help him. He found the master, a simple old man walking along a path carrying a large bundle of firewood on his back. The seeker asked him: 'How do I become completely free?' The master eyed him intently and put down the bundle he was carrying. He didn't say a word. Time passed. The seeker impatiently asked: 'Is that it? Then what?' The master picked up his bundle, hoisted it on his back and continued on his way.

Our burdens can seem very difficult to put down. We keep trying to fix things and control events. The result is often more rainbows to chase, further goals to pursue with an increasing sense of futility - they fail to bring real peace or make a radical difference. Putting down our burdens isn't just a matter of wishing to drop them, nor of imagining they have been dropped, nor of denying them, or escaping from them into belief systems or distractions. We need something else. As Einstein said: 'You can't solve problems with the same mind that created them.' We need some help because the stress is so integral to our life that when trying to clean it, we find we are always washing ourselves with dirty water.

What is the source of these teachings?

The Buddhist teachings are a vast resource of refined and clearly developed sets of tools to transform the way we experience life. There is something extraordinary and awe-inspiring about these teachings. They have been developed over millennia yet remain well-preserved, easily transportable and adaptable, highly practical and direct. We do not need to carry out onerous intellectual archaeology: digging for the treasure under layers of interpretations, ritual, special languages, commentaries and control by a priesthood. Other sacred books and teachings, such as the Judeo-Christian Bible or the Hindu Upanishads, are rich resources of knowledge, but at the same time accounts of events and myths. In contrast the thousands of Buddhist texts, called suttas, are all basically instructional, giving a myriad of simple and direct tools for living with *Wisdom*, joy and freedom.

Such teachings and practices have been trickling into the modern world from the monasteries of the East for not much more than half a century. One sign of their arrival is that they have become an integral part of the culture. For many of us, the gateway to these teachings is *Mindfulness*. This has become a hugely popular personal resource in the last few years, reaching into hospitals, prisons, schools, European parliaments and psychology clinics. One personal example: since September 2016, I have been invited to dozens of bars and pubs for sessions we have titled 'Buddha at the Bar', talking to and engaging with thousands of people who are struggling to find meaning and offering them new ways to look at their lives. To me, this is an indication of the thirst for another, more insightful and transformative way of looking at life. It is also an expression of how these teachings are no longer esoteric but are fully available within our culture.

The Five Powers: going beyond mindfulness

There are many qualities, methods, spiritual paths and practices in the world's spiritual heritage. Were we to ask teachers from different traditions what basic teachings and practices they would recommend to help us in our inner journey:

- A Buddhist monk might prioritise *Mindfulness* and Awareness
- A Hindu swami might say: *Calm* and Concentration
- An inspiring philosopher would call for *Wisdom* and Insight
- A Tibetan lama might suggest Faith and *Trust*
- A psychologist could encourage Positive *Energy*

However, we don't need to collect these key tools from diverse paths and cultures. They are already here, compiled and available in the Buddhist teaching of The Five Powers: highly developed, extraordinarily effective, sophisticated and yet crystal clear. *Mindfulness* is just one of the five. The other four are equally powerful and effective, but less often examined.

These are The Five Powers, along with their original name in the Pali language, the language of the ancient texts, regarded as the original teachings of the Buddha.

1. *Trust, Faith, Confidence* - **Saddha**
2. *Energy, Aspiration, Determination* - **Viriya**
3. *Mindfulness, Presence, Awareness* - **Sati**
4. *Calm, Serenity, Concentration* – **Samadhi**
5. *Wisdom, Insight, Awakening* - **Pannya**

In various traditions, such as the Indian chakra system, these powers also have corresponding colours. White is *Trust* because it is the great embrace, the big heart, which includes all the colours of the rainbow. Blue is mindful awareness, like the still waters and the ocean within. Green is *Energy*, the growth, creativity and abundance of nature. Red is the steadiness and base of the earth, the colour of the root chakra. Yellow is the power and purity of interconnected *Wisdom* like the rays of the sun that shines on all, or incorruptible gold.

When these powers are not yet developed, they are traditionally described as The Five Spiritual Faculties. As capacities they are given a high status in the Buddhist teachings and are part of a list of human abilities that are described in Pali as Indriya, from the Sanskrit name of the chief Vedic God Indra, indicating both their divine quality and their life-changing potential. These are virtues that we all already possess and manifest to some extent. In Bhikkhu Bodhi's words: 'appearing initially in mundane roles in our everyday lives... as trustful confidence in higher values, as vigorous effort towards the good, as attentive awareness, as focussed concentration, and as intelligent understanding. The Buddha's teaching... transforms these commonplace mental factors into spiritual faculties, mighty instruments in the quest for liberation that can fathom the profoundest laws of existence...' When these five faculties are developed in this way, they become transformative powers, Bala in Pali.

The Five Powers work together to amplify and empower each other. Each is required to achieve a complete and harmonious whole. They have been described as five horses working together to skilfully draw the carriage of our being to states of contentment and liberation. *Mindfulness* is the lead horse, showing the way. Behind it, *Trust* and *Energy* are paired and then the two steeds of *Calm* and *Wisdom*. It is obvious that these powers need to be balanced. For example, faith without *Wisdom* can lead us blindly into unfounded and unwise beliefs, illusions and expectations; while *Wisdom* without a trusting heart can lead to an excessively analytical, conceptual and judgemental mind. *Calm* without *Energy* can lead to passivity and laziness; but *Energy* without *Calm* and concentration leads to agitation and a grasshopper mind. Without *Trust*, *Calm* and *Mindfulness* can be mechanical and limited; *Trust* without *Calm* can lead us to fruitlessly chase the rainbow. *Mindfulness* is the lead horse throughout the journey because it will show us how to work with all the powers in a balanced way.

We may find that we have a greater inclination, or are more naturally gifted with respect to one or more of the faculties. We may inherently be more curious and alert, calm and serene, vigorous and energetic, reflective and wise, or heartful and devotional. The traditional advice is to work with and develop whichever quality is easiest for us: this can take us far and show us great possibilities, while the other powers can be recruited along the way.

The Five Powers work together to amplify and empower each other. Each is required to achieve a complete and harmonious whole.

Let's take a walk up the mountain

There is a temptation to regard these powers as inner muscles that we need to develop, as if we are going to some sort of spiritual gym that will help us succeed and get on in life. Our motivations, like the impetus that drives much of the current interest in *Mindfulness* practice, may be for immediate benefits. In principle, there is nothing wrong with aspirations such as these. It is completely understandable to want to be, for example, a better manager, therapist or accountant. Indeed, there are great spiritual teachers who started their journey by going to a monastery because they wanted to deal with some acute problem such as stress or headaches. But that should be just the beginning.

As our practice develops limited goals are extended and refined. Just as when you ascend a mountain, the motivations for your climb may evolve as you progress. At the start of the climb, you may simply want to clear your head or address a particular issue or problem that is bothering you. As you continue on your way, you enter into the swing of things, the joys of the open road: for the first time you notice the delicate blue flowers lining the path, you may become motivated by curiosity and interest in the world around you. Ascending further, you lift your head and wonder at the grandeur of the clouds.

In the same way, as one treads the path of self-discovery and development one comes to glimpse one's own inner beauty and potential. That's when motivations can transmute from the palliative to the more expansive: psychological freedom and well-being, and, as the path leads us ever on, a spiritual longing for total freedom. Eventually that too dissolves. There is no need for any motivation based on the wish to be somewhere other than where and who we really are. The mountain vanishes and climbing is the same as being.

Let's stay with this analogy. What do The Five Powers feel like on our journey and how do they help us climb? *Mindfulness* helps us to notice where and how we are on the path and to discern the rocks and flowers along the way. As awareness and inner freedom expand, we are no longer mired in the issues, limitations and obstructing tribulations of daily life. Heart-opening *Trust* and confidence support our body and mind, bringing hope to the climb and faith in the view. *Energy* and motivation help us to skip rather than crawl. Serenity and concentration keep us steady and focused, so we don't wander off, give up or become overly distracted. And *Wisdom* is all the things we learn on the way: from the understanding of our capacities and limitations, to precious insights and realisations; from a deep silence and sense of oneness with the mountain, to the glory of the sunrise at the top.

As we explore each of these teachings, it may be helpful to keep at the back of the mind the idea that there is a much bigger context to these qualities and powers. The Five Powers are embedded in a rich kaleidoscope of Buddhist teachings working together - a great ecological field of liberating insights and practices. While we cannot take on the vast body of all the teachings in one fell swoop, we do need to be curious and open to the hints that might arise as you read this book. For example, a basic understanding of The Five Powers may at first see them as qualities that we develop within ourselves. However, we might come to realise that the harmony and purity of our actions and our heart in relation to the world are an essential support and grounding for practice. This, in turn, could lead us to consider and explore how the Buddhist teachings include ethical sensitivity as a basis for personal development.

The way I have described and explored The Five Powers in this book is an expansion of their very precise Buddhist definitions, which usually involve a formulation of specific methods of spiritual practice. The word 'saddha' for example, in its traditional sense means faith or conviction.

I have extended it to include *Trust*, acceptance, confidence, and even a touch of love. The usual way samadhi is understood and practiced in the tradition is as concentration and meditative focus. But I have extended it to include serenity, *Calm*, and steadiness. In fact, a broader understanding of these powers is included in the tradition as a description of the fruits of practice, not just the practices themselves. It implies a way of life in which practice and the fruit of practice merge together. For example, the fruit of the practice of samadhi is portrayed as the serene presence of those that center themselves in calm, concentrated attention.

It is important to realise that these powers are relevant to all of us: we don't need to be card-carrying members of the Buddhist club. The Buddha himself taught qualities, tools and a view of reality, and specifically stated that they should be adapted to whatever culture, environment, and language was appropriate. The Buddha was not a Buddhist. The Five Powers are in the end a toolkit for transformation, for a liberated life, not a set of principles or distant ideals. If we live them, we will gradually become them and manifest them in thought, word and deed. This will utterly transform both ourselves and the world around us.

The First Power

Trust

Saddha

TRUST | FAITH | CONFIDENCE

why is trust
so important?

It is Trust that empowers us to embrace life rather than constantly struggling against it. Instead of shutting our doors, we can fling them open to let in any and all the guests that come knocking – even those who are somewhat challenging. It is Trust that helps us to rejoin others and rejoice with them, to reconnect ourselves to our world. It is an attitude that welcomes experience and allows things to be the way they are.

It is possible for us to develop a trusting heart with which to engage fully with life, opening up to joy, positivity and love. By reducing our own basic insecurity, we transform the tension, aggression and conflict in our world. With Trust, we step easily along the path to transformation and inner freedom. We do not succumb to helplessness and uncertainty. Trust gives us the strength to explore the uncharted territories of our spiritual life.

Trust is traditionally listed as the first of The Five Powers. This is because we need to be able to relax a little, to reduce the level of anxiety and concerns just enough so as to practice and explore the other powers. It would give us the space and ease to apply a little effort and motivation, the second power of Energy, which leads to the third power namely the practice of Mindfulness.

It is hard to begin to develop Mindfulness if there are too many ants in our pants and bees in our bonnets. A primary instruction of teachers of Mindfulness, whether today or at the time of the Buddha, would be to enter a safe space and to some extent reduce fretting for or about the world. This would then permit settling down and collecting ourselves into the here and now.

A readiness to welcome whatever life brings is essential equipment for our inner journey. Our initial motivation, whatever it is, will help us take the first steps forward, but what we need to keep going is Trust. It is an engine that drives transformation by constantly clearing the path, sweeping away lack of confidence, paralytic doubt or hopelessness.

is life just about coping?

This might seem quite a mission. We might be forgiven for thinking that life is an endless struggle. Indeed, when we look closely, even when things are OK, the mind is in a state of mild anxiety about what might happen and what needs to be taken care of. Something in us is looking for trouble. Ever watchful of where the next threat

might be coming from, we get bored with easiness, inactivity and well-being. The mind is constantly spinning to-do lists, coping strategies, ways to have enough money, to get what is needed, to be healthy, to be liked, to prevent failures, to avoid conflicts and so on. We try to control life, to make sure we are comfortable and stay that way, but in the end we fail. We are not and cannot be in control of life, so the task is endless and finally, fruitless.

This insecurity turns inwards as well as outwards. Our own voices of self-criticism, self-judgement and self-doubt may run the show, driving our actions. We are pushed to be competitive, to do better than others, to seek praise and recognition, to measure ourselves against arbitrary standards, such as how much money our peers have. It makes us feel that there is an unfillable hole inside us and that we are constantly missing something. It is as if there is a running commentary that says: 'this too is not enough'.

Can we somehow live with more ease? Can we dance with changing circumstances? Can we welcome life even if it is uncontrollable? Can we let go of the endless need for things to be better or a certain way? What would it be like to live like that? Is it at all possible? How do we do it? Trust is part of the way.

how can trust
calm our fears?

Trust silences those voices of concern and replaces them with voices of well-being and harmony: the car will get parked; the day is welcoming. We don't need to work so hard to protect ourselves, to build and maintain our shields and defences, to try to predict what might go wrong. We can let go and let life carry us. We are on the train of life, so why do we need to keep lugging the heavy baggage of our concerns? Why don't we put them down and let the train carry us and our luggage? We can trust the world, because even though it will throw pleasant and unpleasant circumstances and surprises at us, it is neither against us nor for us: it is completely with us. Knowing that, we can relax into what arises and end the struggle.

Trust is an attitude that can accompany us in our everyday life, facilitating, welcoming and sweetening every interaction and contact with others or with events. The way we look at things determines the way things seem to be. If we start our day with anxiety, everything we meet feels threatening and so justifies the fear. A thief will only see pockets, as the saying goes. By the same token, if we arise with Trust, we will see it everywhere: in the smile of the shopkeeper, in the eyes of passers-by in the street. As our Trust radiates, it will tend to bring out ease in others. They too feel its sweetness and tend to respond in the same way. It is true that if we are in an Eastern market, Trust might make things a little more expensive than caution! But it's worth the extra: we will feel much richer by living with Trust.

what is primal trust?

We are born with primal Trust as well as primal fear. I was always astonished at how easily my grandchildren were able to fall asleep in my arms or those of a stranger when they were babies. As we grow to adulthood, the Trust gets squeezed. Though buried under layers of threats, wounds, and disappointments, that inner sanctuary is still there. We can still feel primal Trust within the womb of life, which nurtures us. It appears to us, almost by surprise: in moments of love, in the joy of a stroll in the forest, the aroma of a cup of good coffee, a game with our kids.

A readiness to welcome whatever life brings is essential equipment for our inner journey

unblocking
the trust channel

Like all The Five Powers, Trust is developed in two main ways: by recognizing and clearing the obstacles and blocks to it, and by appreciating and developing it as an attitude and experience. Let us start with recognising and clearing the obstacles.

The tool we use to recognise the obstacles – the fears, anxieties, habits, and addictions that intervene in our encounters with circumstances – is Mindfulness. We can learn to observe – with care, attention, and kindness – how reactivity and defensiveness arise in the face of an experience we perceive as threatening. Locate them in the body, perhaps as a contraction in the belly. See them as phenomena that arise by themselves, triggered by conditions and then change and disappear like bubbles. The key is to identify them but not identify with them. We will explore Mindfulness in detail in a later chapter.

If we take a step back from the chain of responses to a threatening situation, we can watch scenes unfold in the mind as a fever of strategies, justifications and resentments that take over the stage. We keep tracking the whole show as it develops, changes, and dies away. The seemingly impenetrable thicket of responses and reactions miraculously opens up to us if we plunge into it with awareness and interest and we pass through quite easily. When anger between people is dissolved and transformed into the relief of humour or an embrace, there may be more Trust and closeness than before the fight.

A social worker once described to me the pervasive fear, tension and stress she felt every day when she needed to go to work through a part of town that was largely populated by North Africans. I suggested that she could re-label this fear as a sensitivity to conditions and influences, a sensitivity preferable to indifference and denial, something that can be looked at as it arises and as it passes. She needed to befriend it, give it life and space, not blame herself for it, but watch it as it passed by without getting caught in the movie. Gradually, the fear would resolve, perhaps changing into interest. When I met her some time later, she said that she now regularly stopped for a cup of tea, sat with the locals, had developed a relationship of Trust with them and enjoyed their vitality and friendliness.

The way we look at things determines the way things seem to be

what is the behavioural option for developing trust?

When we are faced with daily life situations that make us insecure, anxious or defensive, we want the disturbing fear to go away. We might develop 'safety behaviours', such as withdrawing into screens or mobile phones or into a 12-hour working day. Or we may project the emotions out to others as irritation, nervousness, argumentativeness, defensiveness and so on. This gives authority to the insecurity and strengthens its hold.

As we shall see, Mindfulness will expose the fear and give us a handle on it. But we should also reduce our investment in it and the behaviours that it creates. One way to do this is to get into the habit of acting as if there is no fear: 'fake it till you make it'. If you are confronted by someone challenging or unpleasant, initiate the conversation. If you are afraid to go into a cold swimming pool, just put your toes in without thought. If you are insecure about public speaking, just start talking as if to a close friend in a café. This is acting as if we have more Trust than we actually feel. It is also inviting Trust to be our partner in life. Act as if you trust life and you soon will.

Once I was deep in a dry river valley in a nature reserve, sitting on a rock and meditating. Suddenly there came a tremendous crashing from the bushes nearby; it sounded as if there was a monster in there. The next moment, a wild boar the size of a donkey emerged from the thicket and walked straight towards me. Fear arose. Suddenly I remembered the advice from the Buddha: whatever position you are in when fear arises, just maintain that pose. (of course, not when you are in the path of a London bus, but most fears don't require us to jump out of the way). I decided to follow this advice, and stayed sitting quietly on the rock with legs crossed, without letting fear run the show. The boar sniffed my feet and wandered off. I felt relief of course, but also a sense of deep harmony with the boar and with all life.

how to
develop acceptance

Acceptance builds Trust. It is the precise antidote to withdrawal behind the walls of protection, defence, and concern. The Buddha used the parable of a man wounded by a poisoned arrow: suppose that man should decide that he would not let the arrow be removed until he had a full report as to who shot the arrow, the kind of bow used, the material the arrowhead was made from and so forth. 'That man,' said the Buddha, 'would die without knowing any of these things.'

Let us therefore reframe acceptance as a deep attitude of allowing things to be the way they are. This is Trust. It is not giving in or giving up, but giving permission to both pleasant and unpleasant experiences. Rather than resisting and struggling, we take charge by engaging, by turning towards experience with sympathy and care. Acceptance, in the form of Trust, helps us to remain steady and connected with what is happening and so find wiser ways to respond. Acceptance can even be a prelude to joy and appreciation.

We build Trust by practicing acceptance again and again. We can do this as a meditative practice, in which we locate and recognise an unpleasant experience. Be it physical pain, emotional difficulty, a disturbing noise or failure, turn towards this challenging experience as a gift from the present moment. Instead of labelling it as a problem, we see it as an expression of nature, as part of our life at this unique instant. We listen to its voice like a mother listening to her child.

By looking carefully at our fears, challenges and insecurities, and embracing them just as they are, we can achieve precious moments of learning and inner freedom. We can welcome these difficult external events as messengers from beyond, as our teachers revealing to us where we need to put our attention, see things differently and take responsibility.

Act as if you trust life, and you soon will

re-imagining
our demons

We can also practice reframing our experiences in a radically different way. For example, we can see a series of judgmental thoughts as just a cacophony of voices from the past; obsessive mind states that are just loops in the brain chugging along in the background. We can define them as disturbing external noise, as simply sound waves flowing through the air. A feeling of being a bit depressed can be perceived as a weight on our shoulders that we can put down; a body pain as the fretting of an inner child; an experience of failure as an ink blot in our journal.

Perhaps you can try this exercise. Imagine a recent situation of unpleasantness, disturbance or stress, such as being caught up in a dispute with someone close. Go back over the scene in detail; what was said at the time, what clothes you were wearing, what the surroundings looked like, what position you were in, etc. Be aware of both verbal and emotional scripts. Now imagine that you radiate a wave of awareness and acceptance through yourself, allowing and observing the stress in the body, seeing the emotions as energy passing through the system, looking behind the eyes of the other person to sense their stress and inner pain. Be aware of how the situation arose naturally as a result of the conditions that led to it, automatic reactions in which both of you were entrapped and not entirely the fault of either one. Sense a heartfelt sympathy or compassion for both of you caught up in this painful situation. Now imagine how the event might have unfolded differently with that understanding. Rewrite the script accordingly.

We can turn to face the demons that chase us and see that they in fact are our own sweet selves, all dressed up in the clothes of our psychological wounds, our insecurities, and painful memories.

Another way to build Trust is to shift perspective from myself as the subject, victim and owner of my experience, to a larger, more expansive view. The Biblical Book of Job tells the story of how one man, Job, gradually succeeded in making this shift.

Most of the Book of Job describes, in beautiful and poetic language, Job's determination to understand why good people suffer and his often-furious rejection of all kind of moralistic, rational and social explanations. His persistence was eventually answered in a revelation that the question was the problem, because it came from a place of personal expectations, interests and ego. He was given a deep vision of life, which was not interested in what Job expected from it and was utterly wild, mysterious and uncontrollable: the way the mountain goat gives birth or the hawk turns in the air and the whales cavort in the ocean. He understood that the only way to live was to surrender to the big picture and accept and Trust life as it is. Trust is divine, awesome, coming directly with the voice of the ultimate ('God').

The story also reminds us that our life can be sacrificed to our expectations. We can be endlessly serving our expectations of the way things should be, of what we want from life or from others or, as in the case of Job, views that we hold on to. The modern world is collapsing under the weight of unsustainable human expectations. Can we watch life with amazement rather than expect it to be a supply source?

karma: socializing with the big K

Karma, the principle of causality, is an Eastern concept that could invite us into an easier embrace of life's ups and downs. It is neither a comforting belief system nor another linear explanation based on reward and punishment. Rather, it is a liberating insight into reality as a huge web of interacting influences that makes us and the world as we are. It gives us our mental and physical shape. Karma offers an opportunity to let go of the pressure of taking everything personally and needing to control things. In a sense it is all happening by itself. Yet there is a personal aspect, as we influence life and life echoes our choices and intentions back to us. But be careful! If we go too far with the view that life is just impersonal wheels turning, we can feel resigned and disempowered. If we go too far with 'as you sow, so shall you reap', we fall into reward and punishment and the blame game. We need to hold the impersonal and personal together.

There is a Tibetan saying: 'Keep your vision as wide as the sky, but sieve your actions like fine flour'.

how can I trust
in this world?

So, we belong to the world, we are part of it. We are not an isolated entity watching it from a distance. Outside and inside are in a constant dynamic relationship. Every breath we take, we breathe in the outbreath of the forests, every bit of food we eat is the result of the sun, the earth, the rain, other people's effort. Every drop of water in our bodies has been in the rivers, the clouds, the rain and in other people's bodies. We are constantly forming ourselves from what comes in and out of us. The world and us are part of each other. If we really see that, how can we not trust the world? Surely it would be a bit like not trusting our own hands?

This may seem confusing. How on earth can I trust the world if it is full of cataclysms, tsunamis, devastating storms and the fearful build-up of global warming? How can I trust an environment that at any moment will attack me with viruses and bacteria, make me sick and miserable in countless ways and to cap it all, will certainly kill me off in the end?

The answer is that we have no real choice. The struggle to control things, anxiety about what might happen at any moment, fears for the future, are in the end a far more painful, costly and

It is not giving in, or giving up, but giving
permission to both pleasant and unpleasant
experiences

disturbing way to live. Instead, let us view these threats as nature responding in the way it knows and let us trust it to do so.

Climate change is the planet responding in the way it knows to what we are throwing at it. The symptoms of a sickness are mostly the body reacting as it can, to try to deal with pathogenic influences. Psychological pain is mostly the result of voices and actions of others, such as parents, that invade the consciousness and stay there. Our scars are the result of conditions that have arisen and we do not need to blame ourselves and take it personally. If we want, we can blame Samsara, the Wheel of Life, instead. If we look at things from a more inclusive universal place, reducing the tendency to feel a victim of circumstances, our Trust in the world will be restored. We can trust life to do what it knows.

Trust works, even in difficult circumstances

how can trust drive successful action?

Surely, we need our ambition and drive? Where would we be without competitiveness? In the Stone Age, not the Internet Age. When challenge, concern and opposition are such powerful agents of change and success, doesn't Trust make us wonderfully relaxed, but amazingly unsuccessful?

How can Trust drive successful action? On one level, it is obvious that Trust helps things to work. If we don't trust the body to function, it will start to complain: the digestive system will grumble with indigestion, the heart will nervously miss beats, the back muscles will be tense and seize up and the immune system will attack us instead of defending us. The same for the body politic: we have to trust each other for society to work. And, of course our children can go way off course if we don't trust them. Here too we can see the importance of Mindfulness and Wisdom as they work hand-in-hand with Trust. Mindfulness enabling us to develop an awareness and instinct for what can be trusted beyond blind faith, while Wisdom guides us towards a bigger view of ourselves and how we trust our connections with the world.

It is true that sometimes righteous anger, challenge and even fear can recruit a powerful energy and produce remarkable achievements. But this comes at a cost. In the long term, such adrenaline-fuelled motivation is unsustainable and results in stress, burnout and disappointment. So many activists end up exhausted and despairing. Besides, these emotions are not exemplars of the beneficial outcomes we struggle to achieve. The meeting rooms of peace organisations are often noisy with dispute. Instead, if you wish for peace, be peaceful. The peace walks which I led in the Middle East made an impact in their time because the Israeli and Palestinian, Jewish and Arab participants embodied and radiated Trust and peace while walking slowly and quietly together. So, on another level, Trust allows much smoother, sustainable and authentic actions and outcomes.

how trust can
help your business

Trust can work better in the end, even in difficult circumstances. The corporate world is the symbol of bottom-line thinking, competitiveness and pressure. But it is already well-known and proven that companies work better and employees are more productive, loyal and successful in a climate of Trust rather than suspicion, clock-watching and pressure.

How do you prune a tree? Do you attack the branches you want to cut back as enemies or do you look at each branch carefully, sense its expression, listen to its song and then shape the tree just right? Trust works, even in difficult circumstances. I had a friend who was a highly experienced Company Manager (CEO) and was often brought in to turn around loss-making corporations. He had a quietness and a remarkable ability to listen to everyone without distinction, from the executives to the cleaners, puffing gently on his pipe. He was modest, did not demand monstrous bonuses for himself and was able to generate an atmosphere of Trust in the company. This way he drew the best out of people and encouraged fidelity. If he had to wield the hatchet, he did so with care, clarity and consideration.

The world and us are part of each other.
If we really see that, how can we not trust
the world? Surely it would be a bit like
not trusting our hands?

Socrates was clear: 'Beware the barrenness of a busy life.' We are a driven society. What tends to dominate our minds? Outcomes that we wish to achieve, judgements of how we are doing, self-created milestones, issues of success and failure, pressure to get somewhere, to-do lists and an intensive busyness. All of this is fuelled by a basic dissatisfaction of where we are, who we are and what we have. There is a deep lack of contentment.

We would be a lot happier if we understood that we can trust things to be the way they are because that is the way they happen to have turned out. With that realisation, we act wisely in the world. With an attitude of Trust and acceptance, rather than a restless need for something to be other than what it is, we can go out and make a difference. The emphasis and attention will be different; much more on how we do things rather than measuring outcomes. The quality of our actions becomes more interesting than the results. If our actions and speech embody Wisdom, clarity, kindness and presence, then it is all worth it. We may actually be more successful, just in different ways. The path, rather than our imagined outcomes, becomes the goal. We don't need to chase rainbows; just enjoy their kaleidoscopic radiance.

Try this in daily life: in front of the computer, on the way to the supermarket, in a meeting at work, in trying to achieve any task. As soon as we notice how much we are chasing goals and outcomes, we can stop, take a breath, take stock, and feel how the need for a result puts pressure on our heart, mind and sometimes body. Laugh, let go and come back into the now. Ask ourselves what are the qualities that I manifest at this moment and listen for an inner response. Then carry on from a new place. Try it out in the challenge of being stuck in a traffic jam. We can be boiling with frustration that all our carefully laid plans have been stymied or we can sit back and enjoy a good break from the illusion of control. There is nothing we can do now, so we might as well let go and choose rest not rage.

trusting the process

The whole issue of means versus ends becomes much more nuanced and paradoxical in our spiritual life. I almost wrote spiritual development, but this already assumes something needs to be developed that was not there before and so already takes a position. Whether it is yoga, meditation, Aikido, Qi Gong, Advaita, prayer, intensive sports or just the search for happiness and well-being, there will be a spectrum from hard work to resting in perfection, from trying to get somewhere to being where we are, from a hard slog up the mountain to parachuting down it from above. In fact, all journeys are a dialogue between time and timeless, path and pathless, road and landscape, between travelling and being.

Generally, at the beginning of a transformative process our motivation comes from the regular mind, which is oriented towards achievements. It measures progress, looks for milestones and compares itself to others. But as the journey continues, both the experiences and the motivations get a bit more refined and more time is spent looking at the view, not just thinking about the goal. As we continue, what arises in the moment

becomes the purpose, rather than what we can get out of it. Effort transmutes into effortlessness and letting things go. It's 'The Zone' in marathons, meditative concentration or Zen in the art of archery. We will find ourselves in this new and more existential place only when we let go of the path and the conditions that brought us there: such as belief in a doctrine or dogma, or the view that we need to be different from who we are, or dependence on a consensus or authority figure or text. Trust is an invaluable ally that can take us to a more existential place. When we know that we cannot 'get' truth but that truth

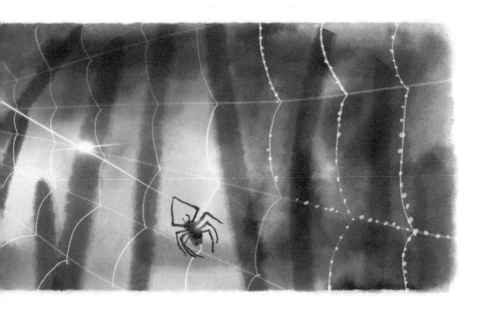

will find us, we can sit peacefully in the shade of a tree by the side of the road.

We can trust the process to do its job, rather than restlessly measuring results. We can have confidence that we are on the path for good or bad. 'The path is wiser than those that walk on it' is an old Chinese saying. Let it take us. If we get stuck in a habit of striving to be somewhere else or someone else, Trust shows us that there is nowhere to go other than where we already are. For example, happiness is an inherent part of our being. We may find ourselves constantly trying to undo the psychological patterns and habits that seem to block it. This can be helpful up to a point. However, we may realise that the more we hunt for happiness the more it hides and when we trust it to show itself, suddenly it is there before us, shining and laughing.

At the very heart of Trust, in the secret core
of our connections to ourselves and others,
lies love

how can I reach beyond hope and trust the way things are?

When we are hopeful, we tend to trust that things will turn out OK. This is definitely a positive state of mind, equivalent to hope. Hope sweetens our life and is an antidote to negative states such as depression, despair and resignation. Cheerfulness is the mark of a developed person. But there are limitations to this Trust because we are not in control of life. Life is in control of us. Hope is conditional. It is hope in something better. But life has other plans. It might not be better and might not turn out OK, and then what? Will we doubt, or think that we failed or crash?

A more sublime form of Trust is trusting things to be the way they already are. This might sound strange at first, but think it through. Our wishes for things to be a certain way are subjective, personal, human and changing. We respond to what happens to us with our needs and wishes. The stock market crashes and we cry, the market soars and we laugh. But if we let go of our personal interests and zoom out, we see that things happen as a result of the multiple conditions that created them, independent of us. Thus, things can't really be different from the way they turned out. We impact the way things will turn out, but our efforts are a response to the situation and just another part of the picture. As Shunryu Suzuki reminds us, 'Everything is perfect, and there is always room for improvement.'

Things happen by themselves. Do we need to command our blood to circulate and our stomach to digest food? We think we control what we eat, but that is a moment of choice and the minute it goes through our mouth we have to trust our digestive system to do its job, our heart to pump and our liver to process. When we are sick, trusting our healing power, the therapists, doctors and remedies help us to get better. Obviously, we need to take care that we get the right medicine or therapist and we need to look after ourselves. But this too can be done with an attitude of Trust rather than worry.

There is an old Zen story about a man standing on a bridge over a massive waterfall. He noticed a little old man strolling along the path near the falls. All of a sudden, the old man jumped into the waterfall. The onlooker was shocked and ran down to see if he could rescue the old man. As he neared the falls, he was amazed to see the old man emerging on the other side and casually walking away. He caught up with the old man and asked how on earth he had managed to survive. The old man replied. 'Easy, the water went this way and that,', he said, waving his hand, 'And I just went this way and that with it, and found myself on the other side.'

Listen to the music of the grasses, the trees, the animals and other people; to our thoughts; to our heart. We need to trust life enough to receive it, to take it in, to be close to it. There is a perfection in the way things are, even if sometimes they appear inconvenient to us.

loving and being loved

At the very heart of Trust, in the secret core of our connections to ourselves and others, lies love. Indeed, Trust is a form of love, in its wider sense. When we turn to ourselves, our thoughts, feelings, perceptions and bodily sensations, we are embracing ourselves. When we turn to others with care and interest, we embrace them. This embrace is love. Take an example of something very small: a bodily tension or stress, such as around the eyes. The moment we pay attention to it and relax it, we are listening to its voice, responding with the attention that the voice is calling for. We trust this voice to tell us what is needed. This care and attention is love.

What blocks love is mostly the inner fears and insecurities of our ego or self. For example, we may love a child, partner, or family member until they don't do what we want, or do not love us back, or get too familiar with others, or hurt or insult us, or become too demanding. Our love can easily turn to anger, jealousy, or other emotions and is held hostage by the challenge to our ego. Our heart meets a limit and is bounded by the needs of the self. Deep and enduring Trust reduces the anxious small voice of the 'me', which says I want to love but cannot because I feel threatened.

How can we unblock the heart? One traditional Buddhist practice is to say phrases internally to change the inner atmosphere. A classic phrase that increases Trust and love would be: 'May I love and accept myself just as I am right now'. Directed at others, it would become: 'May you love and accept yourself just as you are right now'. Another very simple and classic phrase would be; 'May I be happy' or 'May you be happy'. The phrases act as triggers to the heart, shifting it out of its confusion of feelings, resistances and needs into a more open, bounteous space.

Our heart is nevertheless wild with its own agenda, so we should be patient and realise that feeling life can only be tamed gradually, as a wild horse is tamed, with patience, repetition and connection. Allow the phrases above to float up into consciousness repeatedly in the quietness of a meditation session or in a challenging moment during daily life. We can say them a few times and then be still and silent. We may notice and appreciate any changes in our feelings. It is as if the words of Trust and love are stones that we throw into a pond and then watch the resulting ripples.

Of course, we can also practice without phrases or words, using just the silent intention to purify and develop our experience of life in the direction of Trust and love. We can start with feelings that we find relatively easy, such as gratitude and appreciation. They may be connected to a specific event or cause, such as something that we received or that was done for us, but they can be without any obvious cause. In the Buddhist tradition, this is practiced as a vibration that is broadcast to oneself and out into the world in all directions. In the Pali language, the word for this practice is 'metta', which can be translated as 'unlimited friendliness'.

We can take it into every corner of our life and into everything that happens in the world. Metta is also understood as immeasurable love. If we find ourselves emanating love everywhere, it becomes unlimited. It feels like the world is made of it, is put together by love. Every word and action, however difficult, will have love as its driving force. The sun rises and sets, the wind blows, the seeds sprout, life bursts out from everywhere, sending us love letters as it does so.

I was once stopped by a policeman for a traffic offence. As he began to write a ticket, I beamed at him with a lot of metta and asked him how he was and how was his day. 'Not bad' he responded. 'I hope I haven't ruined yours', he said. 'Not at all', I answered, 'That would be impossible'. 'Are you sure?' He responded, 'Even with this hefty fine'? 'Yes, even that cannot spoil my day!' We both laughed. How different this small scene could have been without enduring friendliness.

trust 'works' only when accompanied by the other powers

Trust cannot stand alone. It needs the other powers, otherwise it gets lopsided or taken to extreme behaviours. For example, when Trust or faith is not balanced by Mindfulness, it can lead us to be uncritical, unreflective and credulous. If not also balanced by Wisdom, we can find ourselves in cloud cuckoo land. If Trust is not balanced by Calm, it can lead us to be spaced out or blindly following different opinions, jumping from one bandwagon to another. If not balanced by Energy and motivation, it can lead us to passivity and helplessness, indulging in nice dreams, which can flip into despair when they are unfulfilled.

There was someone I met over several years who was greatly devoted to social change projects. He trusted in the goodness of those around him and indeed inspired them to get together to create a new society based on spiritual values, community projects, city ecological vegetable gardens and so on. But nothing worked for very long because he could not listen to others nor support them and tended to be scattered and distracted, as if his good heart was pulling him to and fro. He wasn't ready to confront the shadow side of himself or anybody else. When others wanted to do things differently he felt betrayed and his inner fire, driven by hope, went out. Trust was there, but it needed Mindfulness and steadiness to accompany it. He started to practice mindful awareness and through this he could begin to see others more deeply, to listen to them, but also to discover in himself suppressed voices of deep pain and lack of love that fuelled an escape into blind idealism. He found his compass.

trust as a bamboo
belief as a rock

For some, Trust may be a bit abstract or subtle. They need a stronger protection, more like a great rock than a bamboo stalk that bends in the wind. There is a rock – belief – which can be immensely powerful in settling the mind and heart and giving us a direction in life. The uncertainties of life may seem resolved in a belief in politics, religious doctrine, ways of thinking, in what many others say, in strong charismatic individuals, in a better future or paradise somewhere else or in cultural and knowledge systems like science. In fact, the uncertainty is merely held at bay, not permanently vanquished.

Belief can temporarily silence a host of nagging voices, often unconscious, that are trying to tell us about our psychological pain. But at the same time it tends to silence the music of life, the richness of inquiry and the gifts of unknown things. There is a quaint folk story about the exclusivity of belief. A man kept playing the guitar at home all day, but he only ever played one note. His wife was in despair. After a month of this she begged him: 'I am going crazy! Stop playing just one note. Why don't you play music like everyone else?' 'Everyone else is looking for the one note,' he answered, 'I have found it!'

6

Faith is a power that can soothe our needy and anxious self but does not exact as great a cost as belief. It is not so attached to an object, a concept, a view, a deity or a social norm and is therefore softer and broader. Faith is much more about placing the heart than selling the soul. It does not require us to suspend judgement and discernment, but adds warmth to them. However dark and difficult our life might be, faith can be like the cracks that let in rays of light, stars that twinkle at us in the night, or the small pilot light in a gas fire, capable of triggering a big warming flame when needed.

In the Buddhist teaching, faith is like a jewel that, when placed in dirty water, clarifies it, clearing up the mental mud and pollution. It gives our mind a direction and a focus on something greater than itself. What drives the process is the heart: the heart is touched by faith, which it then passes on to the mind to weave new helpful insights.

Faith is the sense of deep inner alignment to what matters, to what is significant and beneficial to ourselves and the world. A person who is full of goodness and conviction draws others to them. In the early Buddhist texts, a person of faith is likened to a large banyan tree that welcomes others and gives them a haven or a refuge: 'A massive tree with many trunks and branches, whose branches are full of leaves and an abundance of fruit, there the birds find rest. In that delightful place they

make their home. Those seeking shelter find there shelter, those seeking fruit find fruit to eat'. Does that describe you, or someone you know?

We take 'a leap of faith'. This means that faith allows us to go beyond the limits and the control of the ordinary, the expected, and the habits of mind and heart. It allows us to cross the gap, to sail into uncharted waters or across stormy seas without getting stuck on the shoals of 'what might happen' or shipwrecked on the rocks of anxiety and insecurity. Since real change in our life – indeed, all journeys of discovery – launches us into unfamiliar territory, beyond the usual self that we have grown to know so well, it needs that leap of faith to jump into the new person. The hero's journey is one of our most ancient and enduring myths. Each of us can be that Odysseus that leaves our safe haven and goes on an inner or outer journey of discovery. The first step is always into the unknown, battling difficulties and dragons (usually psychological ones), meeting our true selves, discovering our power and potential and returning home to see it as if for the first time. Trust is the key ingredient that we need for the whole Odyssey.

Faith may seem far away, especially in our modern world, which is so evidence-based, material and functional. Unlike belief, which can be switched on by, for example, a charismatic preacher or a religious group, faith is not so easy to manufacture. We can't just go to the gym to develop our faith muscles. Faith must develop naturally, but we can create the nourishing conditions for it to flower. One way is by the refinement of belief. If we take something we believe in unquestioningly and examine it with kindness, openness and inquiry, it can be like a tunnel of

belief opening out into fields of faith. Many years ago, I used to have quite an extreme belief in ecological living, which led me, among other things, to build my house with hand tools only, as a generator seemed to be 'giving in'. Then I began to realise that such a belief was itself not very ecological nor life-affirming and it softened to faith and Trust in an ecological life, without the obsessiveness.

Faith arises when we are deeply touched by the beauty of something both inspiring and significant. Inspiration, or Wisdom,

significance or sacredness carry us, like the wings of a bird, towards faith. As you read this, can you bring to mind something that really matters, and that is sublime rather than superficial or trivial? For example, a deep teaching or a liberating Wisdom or an embodiment of compassion? Can you really explore your longing for it and at the same time feel it through your being, your mind and heart? Faith will arrive.

In my own case, one of the first triggers to faith were the books of Alan Watts, which combined a vastness of vision with a depth of language and image. Also significant for me were Carlos Castaneda's books recounting his experiences as a student of the Yaqui shaman, Don Juan. Castaneda developed faith in Don Juan when he was able to see for himself the extraordinary powers that lay hidden within the old man.

Faith is validated by the extraordinary, even if it wears the clothes of the ordinary. It can be renewed and confirmed by the awe of a mind-stilling sunset, or the crystal peaks of mountains cutting the sky, or a million shining stars, or the crunch of leaves underfoot in the forest, or by a poem that shakes us to the core. Special experiences occur when faith dissolves the barriers of protection, caution and distance; and draws us closer to the world. We are transported, we feel a deep fulfilment and our faith is confirmed.

the flying trapeze

We make a great effort to know what's going on, to understand the world and our role in it, to make things more predictable and less wild. We raid the vast unknown with an immensely sophisticated brain furiously seeking knowledge and information. But, the unknown in daily life is a constant partner, in the form of a risky venture, a new business project, a new relationship, a spiritual experience, a life change and any journey through uncharted waters, whether external or internal. The unknown is also the territory of liberation, the great wide-open spaces of the unexplored, the unconditioned, the unlimited. However, generally we fill ourselves with the known, keeping the unknown at bay, for it is both compelling and frightening. Primal fear shuts the door to the divine. Primal Trust and faith open it again to mystery and wonder.

The trapeze artist hangs on to one bar and in a heart-stopping moment lets it go and flies through the air before catching the other trapeze. How can we do that - let go of our safe bar, cross the dreaded gap to safely catch the bar on the other side?

It is a training. First, we can start with a little housekeeping: fixing our safety net. We can consider what fundamentals we need so the net is strong and durable. In the Buddhist world,

those fundamentals are both outer ways of life which would include ethical sensitivity, authenticity and steadiness in action, speech and thought; and inner states of mind, which would include kindness, Calm and especially a sense of well-being.

Secondly, we need to change our attitude to the uncertain, to re-label it: no longer is it a terror to be avoided; it is a truth to be discovered. We will understand that the unknown is the world, which is calling to us and beckoning us. If we can meet our vulnerability, we will find ourselves less busy maintaining our comfort zone, becoming sharper, more aware and open to life's invitations.

Thirdly, we practice like a circus performer, again and again, taking risks, in small doses and checking how we feel each time. We need to surrender again and again to the unknown, before arriving again at the safety of the known. We gradually get used to the sense of launching ourselves out into the uncertain and unknown, watching the gut-wrenching sense of insecurity dissolve bit by bit as we welcome and rediscover the nature of primal Trust. All the shifts and passages in life, little ones such as the space between one thing and the next, big ones such as retirement, or major ones such as birth and death, are opportunities to soar fearlessly between one trapeze and the next. 'In order to arrive at what you do not know you must go by a way which is the way of ignorance... In order to arrive at what you are not you must go through the way in which you are not' says T.S. Eliot.

confidence
in the making

Trust and faith bring confidence and reduce our wobbliness, shakiness and uncertainty. Confidence is a precious commodity on the ups and downs of the inner highway. We absolutely need confidence to be able to confirm new understandings or insights. Otherwise, we will undo them as they arise.

A magical thing once happened to me. And I mean it seemed like big magic, not the little magic of daily life. I was on my way to America to participate in a long meditation retreat. I was on the bus from Oxford to London Airport. I shut my eyes and went into contemplation mode, asking myself what I wanted to learn from this retreat. What was my intention? The question reverberated for a while in my mind. The bus was travelling fast. There was the sound of the engine, the constant whine of the tires on the road and the soft sounds of people in other seats talking to each other. Then it came to me. What I really needed was the confidence that it was possible for me to transcend myself. But how could I find that confidence? I didn't know. I opened my eyes and there in huge letters, written along all the windows of one side of the bus was 'CONFIDENCE IN THE MAKING'. I gazed at it in astonishment, especially as the words were unwavering even though the bus was travelling at least 60 miles per hour! After a couple of minutes, the words began to slide forward and I realized they were written on the side of a truck that was now moving a little faster than the bus. The truck belonged to a furniture-making company and that was its slogan. It felt like a divine revelation!

Once a young man came to me in a crisis of confidence. He just couldn't trust his own experience and felt that every thought was unconfirmed, uncertain and unfounded. He was physically shaking. 'What can I rely on?' he asked, on the verge of tears. 'Let's walk together,' I said, and we went outside. We strolled side-by-side for a bit in silence, to shift the energy. 'How are your feet? What are they telling you?' I asked him. 'Do they know what they are doing, what is expected of them?' 'Sure,' he answered. I suggested that he could have confidence in his feet, but also in the ground supporting his feet and himself; in the sky above; in the trees along the way, all of which were just being themselves. I suggested more faith in his body, which also knew what it needed to do. Slowly, step-by-step, we approached the mind and thoughts. I invited him to trust them too, in doing what they knew how to do, receiving and processing the world in the way they did, reporting, expressing, and making their music, just like the trees and the earth.

where is our refuge?

What can we really rely on? Where and how can we find refuge? The usual response would be that we feel really settled when things are going well: when we have enough money in the bank, a comfortable place to live, food in the refrigerator, friends and family who don't fight with us, respect from others and a bright future. But at any moment, any of these conditions can change. Nothing is certain and we may be exiled from our comfort zone. Paradise Past. If we lack Trust, we will be searching endlessly for our real home. If we have Trust, we will be at home everywhere.

We realise that we couldn't find our home, because we were looking out of it.

There is a place that we can feel totally at home, where the conditions of life simply cannot throw us out and which is fundamentally reliable, deep and unchanging; the ocean and not the waves that knock us over. In Buddhist practice it is called

'Refuge' and it is defined as the sense of 'Being', as a basic awareness that we are alive and present. It is the Buddha within. The word Buddha does not refer to a man but is derived from the word Bodhi (in Pali or Sanskrit), which means the awakened mind. Traditionally there are actually two more such Refuges – the Dharma, which means the truth of the way things really are and the Sangha, which refers to others that support our spiritual journey. An image of this in the Psalms is to dwell 'under the wings of the Shekhina,' meaning Presence or the female aspect of the divine.

We find this deep refuge by a constant letting go of what is passing and external. As events come and go, we let them. We constantly say welcome and then goodbye. As we do that, we gradually get a taste of something that does not come and go: the invisible awareness that knows. It may be just for a moment, as we listen to the call of the blackbird under the hedge in the early morning and slip into a quiet space, or a more inclusive sense of being as we walk on the earth and under the sky, or a moment of fresh and unlimited love that opens our heart to everything. We can relish these moments, however short and keep surrendering into them.

What is it that knows and appreciates the stars and a thought, but is not them? It is more of a capacity, a potential, like the womb that is empty but gives birth – to impressions, perceptions, and experiences. This pure and heartful awareness will grow in us as we keep diving into it, finding that it is our true home and begins to feel like a sacred space. We constantly look elsewhere for the Divine. But when we are truly at home, it can find us.

The Second Power

Energy

Viriya

ENERGY | ASPIRATION | DETERMINATION

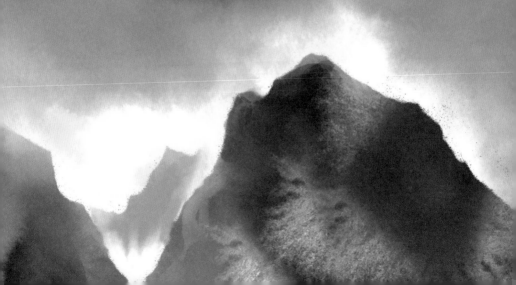

Nothing happens without Energy. If we know how to modulate our Energy and let it take us in its flow, there is no limit to what is possible. This chapter will explore how we can generate the Energy we need and use it as a force for inner and outer transformation.

Energy is multi-dimensional, fuelling all levels of the human being. Vitality, determination, motivation, positive emotions, spiritual elevation and more are all interacting colours in the energetic kaleidoscope. Consider the image of Energy as a tree: physical Energy the roots; psychological Energy the trunk; emotions such as joy, enthusiasm and love are the branches; while spiritual Energy is the crown of rustling leaves open to the sky.

How can we overcome forces such as depression, agitation and hopelessness that deplete our Energy? How do we promote enthusiasm, curiosity, motivation and harmony that enhance it? With the right effort, our Energy can become balanced, steady and inexhaustible, like a constant flame that allows and sustains transformation in the alchemical vessel of our being. Such Energy is helpful in all human situations: whether on the yoga mat or the meditation cushion, when interacting with our loved ones, in front of the computer, at the start of a new project or running a marathon. To use a Buddhist image, we can learn to swim safely across the flood of worldly concerns by neither stopping nor struggling.

Let's make a start by looking at Energy in a general sense. Later in the chapter we will move on to Energy's place among The Five Powers and as part of a path of development and transcendence.

unblocking the energy fountain

Tiredness is the most common of all symptoms that doctors see. We go to bed tired; we wake up tired. We feel drained of vitality. Even if we have enough Energy to make it through the day, that extra spark of joy and enthusiasm is missing. We can do no more than flop in front of the television to recover from the daily grind. The challenges of juggling work, childcare and our other responsibilities may even leave us exhausted, flat and depressed. We lack the Energy to explore our life and relationships, to develop ourselves and to discover new inner and outer landscapes.

One source of tiredness is stress. Stress is not necessarily an issue of direct pressure: it can simply be because of the level of stimulation we experience. If we work all day and switch off in front of the TV at night, there may be too much input besieging our minds and hearts. Best then to shut up shop and allow the inner turmoil to settle. This is external: reducing the level of stress to a level with which we can cope. It needs to be combined with an internal renewal: building inner resilience and Calm. Appropriate habits may include relaxation exercises or a daily walk in nature. Meditation and meditative movement such as Chi Gong – which are discussed at greater length in a later chapter on Calm and Serenity – help us drop into our centre, the place of reset and renewal, where neither we nor the world make demands on us.

Another major source of chronic tiredness is the emotional and psychological patterns with which we confront the world: our worries, suppressed anger, perfectionism, compulsions, guilt and so on. Our inner life, our memories, the scars and hurts and our self-story in all its glory are strong threads that weave a sticky web in which we get stuck. Deep and painstaking work is required to get unstuck. It is psychological work in part, but Buddhist practice offers a great many resources to deal with these pervasive inner constructions. We need to shift our view to reframe these constructions as visitors that come and go rather than as self-evident truths.

We lack the energy to explore our life and relationships

Mindfulness can help us go deeper here. The issues can be explored at the level of the body: for example, as a contraction in the chest that restricts our breath, or as tension in the stomach. They can be clearly observed at the level of the heart as painful feelings and at the level of the mind as thoughts, stories and narratives. The key is to clearly see these experiences as just phenomena that arise and pass away. We identify them, but do not identify with them. As we engage with them, they emerge from the undergrowth and the unconscious and cease to drain our Energy and vitality. Instead of our enemies, they become our teachers and partners in our daily life. Instead of denial, suppression, avoidance

or escape, we embrace them with interest, curiosity, inquiry and openness. Those inner constructions that were previously a source of confusion and anxiety can now enrich us by helping us to meet the underlying themes, even though unpleasant, that drive our life. The waste turns into compost.

A lively, elderly woman, clearly a grandmother, with white hair and a twinkle in her eyes, came to me one day and asked me how to deal with the problem of falling asleep or dozing off during meditation. She said she had been meditating for a long time and it still kept on happening. I told her it is so common as to be almost universal. I suggested that she could take a few deep breaths, stand up and open her eyes, bringing more Energy into the system. However, she needed to see the sleepiness not as a problem but as an invitation, a sign that says 'dig here to find buried treasure'. She needed to be interested and curious about the sleepiness, watching it as much as possible in the present timeless moment: the heaviness, the changes in the mind, the hypnagogic dream-like states and any responses she had to them, the unpleasantness or pleasantness and so on. Attention can open the box to reveal what is hiding there. Perhaps there is fear or anxiety written into the mind-body system. As that emerges, it releases a great deal of Energy and sleepiness disappears to be replaced by insight.

achieving a
healthy relationship

Instead of trying to draw ever more Energy from the well, there is a wiser way. We can develop a sympathetic partnership with states of Energy, understanding their modulations, moment by moment. This intimacy allows us to hear the music of the flow of Energy and to dance with it, so we tune our life more effectively. For example, we can catch that first wave of weariness as it arises and take a ride on it: perhaps take forty winks during the day, or realise that now is the perfect time to go to bed. Without that awareness, we might drive the weariness away with more screen time, paying the price later.

Now we can know when to work in the garden, to exercise, to catch the creative fire and write, or fix the house. If our Energy is taking a dip, we know it is time to read, to rest, or to take a quiet stroll with the dog. We can ride or surf the waves of power within us instead of being at their mercy as they crash down over us. As we do this, we find that our Energy is respected and encouraged and we have more and deeper Energy to play with.

Our body has its own cycles and rhythms. Tracking our Energy states more subtly allows us to maximise our health and prevent stress, burnout, insomnia and dullness.

What's more, if we are in touch with the messages from our Energy source, we can push the boundaries more easily when necessary. Sensing the qualities of our states of Energy can change them. If we are in a long meeting, jogging, teaching, writing, meditating or working in front of the computer and the body and mind spiral into a dip, we may be able to follow this, finding ourselves out the other side. If there are special energetic challenges such as jet lag or night shifts, we may be able to fine-tune the states of energy so that they don't trouble us.

Overall, we will find ourselves empowered by being an aware friend to our Energy rather than its victim.

To recruit our deepest sources of Energy, we need a subtler approach. Think of acupuncture: a tiny hair-like needle, placed in exactly the right place, can unblock a channel of Energy that sweeps through us from head to toe, creating all kinds of functional improvements on the way. The Energy is there, it just needs to be uncovered and released. Energy that flows freely, like a river without a dam, can be dynamic with an animal power. In this way dogs and small children can whizz around like miniature meteors.

We must work to acquire the skill of balancing opposing energies within us. In the traditional Chinese world view, Yang Energy, the active, pushing, dynamic vector is visualized as male, while Yin Energy, the quieter, softer form is seen as female. Yang uses up energy sources, Yin feeds them. If we work with the mind, sitting all day in front of a computer, or equally, if we are talking and communicating all day or busy running about, there is an overload of Yang, an expressive externalization of energy. We might need gardening, walks in nature, deep rest, good nutrition, herbs, Qigong, etc. to replenish our resources and provide the missing Yin. When Yin and Yang are in balance, the powerful Energy of the Shen – spirit or soul – is released. Then, standing outside between the earth and heaven, we can feel lifted by the awe, beauty and love of life. As William Wordsworth said 'with an eye made quiet by the power of harmony, and the deep power of joy, we see into the life of things.'

Balancing the flow between our head and our heart releases huge potential Energy. If we are inspired by something and love what we are doing, we can stay up late into the night without really noticing. Creative fire recruits all the energies of mind, heart and self to achieve the unthinkable. Conviction too, touches the heart, directing the mind and fuelling extraordinary power. Just recently Benoît "Ben" Lecomte arrived in Hawaii after swimming from Japan, a superhuman accomplishment fuelled by the urge to highlight the ecological catastrophe affecting the seas. The power of Trust and faith, as we have seen, can also unblock a great deal of Energy. Compassion and Calm are deep and seemingly endless sources of heart Energy that empower us to help and heal.

A personal example: a few years ago, I began to get up at about four o'clock in the morning with enthusiasm for spiritual practice before the cock crows. That special time when all is deeply and enticingly silent and dark and the dawn is just a seed in the womb of the night. After a couple of weeks, I found to my surprise that the amount of sleep I required dropped from six hours a night to four, the level at which it has remained. My explanation is that the stillness of the practice and days lived in harmony and balance reduced the need for sleep.

Another way of releasing these deeper energies is to bring attention to the subtle yet powerful life forces in our body and mind and give them a helping hand. Ordinary walking becomes an empowering movement. We can experience the Energy body as sensations flowing through us. When resting, we can allow the power of gravity to pull us down and be our friend, letting the earth receive us. We will then rest deeply, even for ten minutes, and arise refreshed.

With sensitive body awareness and Mindfulness, we can feel the flow of Energy through the body, opening and relaxing areas that block the stream. Then we can feel the joy of life running through our veins and tissues. We will dance into our business meetings!

To further enhance our Energy levels, we can also take better care of our physical selves. When I was teaching at Benares Hindu University in India in the mid-1970s, I was exposed to the Indian practical philosophy that food, along with everything else we consume, influences the quality of the Energy of body, mind and spirit. The modern wellness movement may have made this idea more widespread in the West today, but at the time it was a revolutionary concept for me. The idea that foods influence the mind was so fascinating for me personally that then and there I became a vegetarian and have been ever since.

You don't have to become a vegetarian to channel your inner resources, but the right diet – balanced, modest, and wholesome –

Energy that flows freely, can be dynamic with an
animal power

increases harmony, peacefulness, wellbeing and quiet yet powerful Energy. Indulgence in a little of what you fancy is nothing to beat yourself up about but bear in mind that the body and mind benefit from regular cooked meals that are made up of natural unprocessed foods. Look to achieve regularity in quantity and timing, as the body works best when it knows what to expect.

In many Buddhist traditions, dedicated practitioners such as monks do not eat after noontime until the next morning. This leaves ample time for processing and elimination of the food ingested. Such a regimen is not for everyone, but at least try not to eat a heavy meal in the hours before bedtime. Michael Pollan, activist and author of In Defence of Food, suggests that everything he's learned about food and health can be summed up as 'Eat food, not too much, mostly plants.'

Exercise is another key aspect in recruiting Energy and here too the body benefits from regularity. I recently read a bunch of reports showing that apparently the best exercise for helping people to reach an active old age is gardening. This reinforces the astuteness of the Chinese proverb 'To be happy for an hour, get drunk; to be happy for a year fall in love; to be happy your whole life long, cultivate a garden.' This may not be possible for city dwellers, but the principle is important: exercise should lift the mind and the body, should be steady and not over-strenuous and should not be an intensive painful battle with the body in the gym followed by being glued to a chair all day. In addition to gardening, brisk walks or gentle jogging, cycling, yoga, breath work and dancing are all great ways to get the right Energy flowing through the system.

the transformative power of energy

Up until now, we have been discussing Energy in a general sense. But The Five Powers are part of a path of development and transcendence, with Energy, in that context, offering an opportunity for empowerment and growth.

Transformation always requires effort. The chick needs to peck its way out of the egg, the snake must wriggle its way out of its old skin and the butterfly must slowly unwrap itself and unfold its wings from its cocoon. This is the way of growth. Is there something in us that we want to change, or discard, or acquire, or initiate, or a spiritual practice that we wish to develop, or just a wish to somehow shed the old skin and grow a new one? If so, how do we get the drive and Energy for this?

Effort and determination are engines that drive us and release a huge amount of Energy. Think of the lover's tireless efforts to win over their beloved, or the supercharged daily life of someone fired up by strong political or religious beliefs, or the colossal forces expended in fights and battles. Hannibal hauled an entire army on foot across the Alps when he could have been dozing in the sun in North Africa. Ambition will energise the whole system, aligning mind, muscles, hormones, metabolism, heart, identity and soul. There are feisty octogenarian leaders who would otherwise be sunk into an armchair in an old age home.

wriggling out of our old skin

When the time is right, the snake needs to shed its skin, just as we too are faced with going to the next stage in our life. This is natural and yet needs a lot of wriggling. Both easy and difficult. Effort has many forms and we can access more Energy if we know the secrets to refining it. As much electricity can be generated from the tides that move imperceptibly, as from the waves that crash through barriers. Sometimes the hawk needs to flap its wings and make an effort to fly up against the force of the wind and sometimes it simply glides effortlessly, an occasional tweak of a few feathers enough to keep it soaring through the heavens.

We need different kinds of Energy at different times. Energy or effort will be modulated by the way other powers work within us. For example, Trust or faith will encourage a deep and sustainable Energy and reduce the sense of pushing against obstacles. Calmness will create a smoother ride, more like a boat chugging through a gentle swell as opposed to battling billows.

Wisdom will always show us ways to renew our Energy, take short cuts and enjoy the ride. Sometimes we need more thrust to push against barriers visible and invisible. At other times we need a quieter effort, an Energy of poise and persistence. I am amazed to see how my chickens scuttle about frantically pecking and scratching all day with great Energy. They then sit on eggs with extraordinary stillness for weeks, hardly eating or drinking. They channel an equally great Energy into staying power and immovability. Particularly at the beginning of the process of personal development or new directions or practices, we are

likely to need more effort, which is recruited by motivation and determination.

As we keep going there is less resistance and we can coast along. We will explore this subject in the following sections. What is the difference between the thought 'I must make a change in my life' when it surfaces briefly only to disappear within the general imprecise mess of thinking and that same thought on another occasion, when it is like a virus infecting the whole mind and won't leave until it activates us to make the change?

The difference is urgency.

In traditional Buddhist teaching, this urgency for change is called *samvega*. It often comes out of pain and difficulty. The teachings advise that if we experience pain, difficulty and dissatisfaction, it matures either as misery or search. The suffering people that the Buddha met when he ventured out of the opulent hedonism of his palace were retitled 'heavenly messengers' because they kick-started the search for meaning. We can ask ourselves: who or what are our 'heavenly messengers?'

A first heavenly messenger in my own case was Rudyard Kipling! As a child I read *The Jungle Book* again and again. An insight grew within me: if Mowgli thought he was a wolf because he was brought up by wolves, then I only think I am Stephen because I was brought up to think that way. Which means that everything else as well only appears to be as it is because we are brought up to think it is so. So, what is reality? Messengers of this kind kept turning up in my life: among them were Aldous Huxley, Timothy Leary and Alan Watts. Thankfully the British Council helped with the quest by sending me to India to teach at Benares Hindu University in 1976. There, on the banks of the Ganges, the messengers came thick and fast and left me no choice other than the quest. The pain and dissatisfaction inherent in an ordinary existence may be enough to create a search for something else, for the beyond, for 'the above'. The circular round of daily life can feel imprisoning, especially if the social consensus is occupied with conflicts, injustice, materialism, competitiveness, consumerism and the like. We can feel a terrifying sense that we are like hamsters that spend their lives running constantly inside their wheel. Conventional Buddhist or other religions and their priesthoods can depict this as 'Hell' and pump up fear in the audience in order to compel devotion and zeal.

If we experience pain, difficulty, and dissatisfaction, it matures either as misery or search

Many years ago, I participated in a retreat where a Tibetan lama, day after day, graphically described the terrible hell realms that, in the Tibetan tradition, await those who don't practice. Finally, we had had enough. We politely reminded him that many participants were Catholic and had been through all that already in their childhood and he could skip that bit!

For some of us, however, the urgency is engendered by uncontrollable events and the challenge of great suffering: tragic loss, life-threatening illness or closeness to death. We are propelled out of our regular life, our habits and our complacency. The urgency is too real, we need to get answers to save our lives, at least our spiritual lives. And if we heed the call and plunge into a new way of life, we may in the end bless what happened to us, even though we might not wish it on others. More than one cancer patient whom I have worked with over the years has in the end blessed the cancer as a wakeup call that ended a flat life.

how can longing energize us?

The longing for transformation can be dispiriting if we view our life as problematic and miserable, when in fact it is unique and precious. That said, even if there is no conscious idea of what it is that we want, longing can be a beautiful whisper of the beyond, a touch of grace, the call of the unknown, even if we do not yet understand its language. It is like an unlimited or sacred potential within us that confronts the restrictive shell of living in auto-pilot. Determination is a great ally, especially at the beginning of the journey of transformation and realization, for it creates genuine commitment. It is a common misconception that developing our inner life needs just calmness, ease and 'going with the flow'. At times that may be so, but at other times it is too moribund and we need the opposite, for as Jim Hightower warns: 'Even a dead fish can go with the flow'. The spiritual journey needs to be serious, otherwise we will touch it here and there but never really progress: if we want to boil potatoes, we can't keep taking them off the fire. This is especially the case with the search for meaning, which often requires us to sail against the wind of the norm, the consensus, and comfortable apathy. We may need to swim against the current. Is the spiritual journey just a comfortable accessory in our life or is it our life? What are we prepared to give for it?

We tend to go shopping for the right technique and the method or practice that suits us. Whereas it may be more important to follow the longing and the commitment, wherever it takes us, because that is what drives the ship. I once heard the famous Zen Master Harada Roshi answer a question from someone in the audience who said that they practice vipassana, kabbalah, yoga and more and wanted the Roshi's view on his path. The Roshi said: 'It doesn't matter what you do, as long as you practice as if your life depends on it'.

We may not know any way other than to get into top gear and charge at spiritual goals just as we usually do with regular life challenges. We are determined to make headway against the prevailing wind. Determination certainly characterised the way of Prince Gautama before he became the Buddha, after he left his palace. He endured seven years of intense yogic meditation practice and asceticism. Convinced that by beating down the body, its needs and interests he could liberate the mind; he went to extremes. He described how he practised yogic stopping of the breath until he heard a great roaring sound in his ears and his head felt as if it was being pierced with a sharp sword. He starved himself and dressed himself in rags taken from the bodies of the dead. His body became extremely emaciated: he later related how 'on my sides, my ribs stuck out like rafters of a ruined house. My eyes sank so far into my head that they looked like water at the bottom of a deep well, and almost disappeared altogether... If I urinated, I fell over and lay, there... And when I tried to rub my arms and legs to make them feel a little better, the hair on them was so rotted at the roots that it all came away in my hands'. Other great teachers also relate similar heroic journeys, such as the Tibetan sage Milarepa, who for thirty-five years built stone houses on top of hills and tore them down again before his guru Marpa consented to teach him.

Suppose we decide on a new direction in our life: a new skill that we wish to learn; a habit that we wish to dissolve such as anger, anxiety, or guilt; or a practice that we wish to acquire. Our usual response would be to attack it as a project, with enthusiasm and determination, make a lot of effort to succeed and hope to score. It is a natural first try. But are we missing something? Are there more effective ways to navigate?

When we are engaged in inner work, it can often feel hard going. We can't wait for the time we set for our yoga or meditation to be over. We don't have the Energy right now. The experiences themselves may seem flat and uninteresting or we do them on automatic pilot. How can we infuse our practice with more Energy? The classic response is to recruit more determination and renew motivation somehow. But there is another way which is more effective: it is curiosity. If we understand that all spiritual practice is a journey of discovery into what is really happening right now, this can energise our practice just as if we are reading a fascinating book and have to know what's going to happen next. What is my experience in this moment? Where is it heading? What are the voices coming from beyond that I long to hear?

how do we find the middle way?

The emaciated Gautama, sitting by the river, began to realise that he would never reach liberation if he was half dead. He needed the power of a clear and bright mind that would reveal insights, not a weak, exhausted consciousness. So, when a young woman, Sujata, made an offering to him of sweet rice milk, he accepted and ate it. Presently, he heard a party of female musicians passing nearby. They confided that if the strings of their instruments were tightened too much they would break,

while if they were too loose, they could not make music. They needed to be stretched just right.

This experience triggered in Gautama the realization that there is a Middle Way, in which right effort is balanced and healthy; our feminine Energy represented by the gift of nourishment, like mother's milk, balancing the typically masculine principle of striving for success. We have both in all of us and both are needed.

This avoids the extremes of being either hero or zero. The course of the hero, though needed at times to get going against obstacles, can also be violent, obsessive and self-defeating, like beating our head against a brick wall. It can degenerate into a chronic battle against ourselves. The zero way can at times be exactly what is needed to glide along, but all too easily we can fall into illusions, dreams and unrealistic expectations concerning transformation, when actually nothing has really changed.

The duality of too much struggle versus too much relaxation is a model of all the dualities in which we find ourselves caught: this way or that, this side or the other, me or them. Between this and that, a huge space opens up. The realisation of 'not too tight, not too loose' was the last key the Buddha needed to realise ultimate truth. The Middle Way is such an important principle in the Buddhist Path that it became the name for the whole Buddhist way. But it is important to realise that it is not a devotion to compromise, more an acknowledgement that beyond the dualities of hero or zero, either this or that, me and them, inside and outside, mind or body, heaven and earth, there is a vast territory of possibilities and liberating insights. The twentieth century sage Nisargadatta expressed a similar insight in his observation that 'Wisdom tells me I am nothing. Love tells me I am everything. And between the two my life flows.' The Middle Way applies to all The Five Powers. In the case of Trust and faith, there is a wide spectrum between passive acceptance and charged up beliefs. True Calm is the Middle Way between paralysis and heroic concentration practice. Mindfulness certainly treads a dynamic balance between the thinking mind and the heart's intuition, while Wisdom spans the vast range between the analytical and the empty mind. In the case of Energy, it is a wise use of effort that is restrained and harmonious, which seeks out the path of least resistance, but steadily keeps going. It is a soft effort that is kind to us and yet gets there in the end. As in Aesop's Fables, the wise tortoise always seems to arrive at the same time as, or before, the hare. For example, in yoga or exercise or any spiritual practice, it would mean arriving at and recognising an apparent limit and just staying tenderly at the edge for a while without pushing, noticing how the edge dissolves and moves. Supposing we are working on a psychological pattern or tendency such as a fear, anxiety, anger, feeling of being a victim, or self-judgement, the right effort would be to meet the pattern tenderly again and again as it is expressed in mind and body, with soft interested attention. It yields to our embrace, rather than our dismay. Attacking it could create more self-judgement and a lot of troublesome measurement of success and failure.

We saw in the chapter on Trust, as we steadily climb up the mountain to the summit, a relaxed presence takes the place of striving. The quality of Energy and determination changes accordingly. Instead of being driven by immediate goals of what we want to achieve, we take our foot off the gas. What tends to happen is that aspiration takes the place of determination.

We should carefully observe and go with these energetic changes, noticing moments of ease and enjoying them. For example, it may be a little easier to shut up shop in the midst of a busy life for a half an hour of silent meditation if we have been doing it for a while. We may need to grit our teeth a little when starting our jog on a cold morning, but as we keep going, resistance gives way and we can find ourselves happily chugging along. At the beginning of a yogic stretching pose, the ligaments may be grumbling that it is not fair that they are being forced to stretch themselves, but as we stay at that edge, their resistance gives way, they get used to the new situation and both the ligaments and us find ourselves settling into the stretch with ease and even joy.

Aspiration is a long-term process. It is like building a house rather than fixing the plumbing. It is a determination that has softened into an intention that works consistently in the background. It does need effort to sustain it and overcome obstacles on the way, but the rocket has lifted off and is moving out of the atmosphere. It is the shift that happens when we practice regularly, when we have broken old habits and have the confidence that the change is irreversible. Now, the Energy of aspiration is a steadiness that keeps us navigating in the right direction.

At this point, we don't need to think of the journey. Meditation for example, becomes part of our life and we naturally find ourselves aware and present when doing the dishes or changing a nappy. A deep background intention takes over and drives us. We are up there on the mountain and can't go back; we cannot ask to return to ignorance and a state of forgetting. We don't really have a choice. The path has taken us and it requires more surrender than effort. There is a beautiful traditional metaphor of this in a text called the Sutta of the Logs. It says that it is in the nature of logs to float down a river and reach the ocean, unless they get stuck on one bank or the other or become rotten. We reach the ocean of freedom and awakening as long as we don't get stuck on either bank (ourselves and the world's temptations) or become rotten (through ethical blunders). Our individual issues and needs become less important, and intention takes over. At that point, we can call it faith. It is where the power of Trust meets and joins the power of Energy.

The word 'practice' at this point loses its meaning. We no longer hunt for experiences and practice to get better at anything. It is much more like a flower opening because that is the time for it to open. The accumulation of small subtle experiences becomes powerful, yet easy and unhurried, like a small wild plant that can break concrete with its soft persistence. If we seek liberation, all we really need to do is to constantly bend our mind in that direction.

how can we transmute adversity into spiritual progress?

This is a crucial teaching because it invites an Energy that is sustainable, whereas the energy of ambition and the drive for success is dependent on outcomes. It can easily flip over to become despair and resignation if we don't get the results we expect. We can rely on life to be unreliable and expect life to provide the unexpected. Our efforts have to be in line with this, otherwise life may laugh at our ambitions as it overturns them. The way to do this is to keep a sky-wide view. Head towards the horizon, but don't give our goals authority over us. Instead, give the quality of our small actions the authority. If we do this, we will have many moments of harmony on the way. Harmony is the sense that nothing needs to be changed, therefore no effort is needed and at the same time it renews and restores our Energy through the joy of life.

I remember learning this while building my house with my own hands. At the beginning it was an irrational and absurd idea. As a molecular biologist I knew how to work with DNA. But rocks? cement? It was a process that took two years, and many tears of frustration and joy of achievement as I dug rocks from the earth or collected them from the sides of roads and built my house, stone-by-stone. If I wanted to finish a line of stones or was too perfectionist when trying to choose the building stones or if I thought of how much work there was still to go, weakness would invade my muscles. If I let go of all such thoughts and became absorbed in the touch of the stone, its colour and shape, how it lay and fitted its neighbours, how my body could lift each rock if I moved harmoniously – the man working quietly and steadily while the whole of nature looked on – then the Energy kept flowing endlessly. In Greek mythology Sisyphus was condemned to eternally push a stone up a hill and then see it roll back down every single time. The element of tragedy expressed by this myth depends on Sisyphus having a concept of achievement. Without

such a narrative, there was no tragedy. He was simply rolling stones. No problem!

A middle-aged businessman, lively, energetic but with prematurely grey hair and a little thick around the middle, asked to see me during a retreat. He asked me what to do with his need for ambition and drive. He felt that somehow the voices of ambition and success were inappropriate or crude, yet he felt they gave him energy and without them his work and even his life might feel pointless and flat. 'I can't imagine myself without them, and everyone else also tells me I need them'. I reminded him of the donkey that follows the carrot dangling in front of its nose without realizing that is tied to its back with a stick. We create ambition and then follow it, giving it authority, justification and reality, forgetting that it is our own creation. But depending on outcomes is a fragile source of energy. Maybe, I suggested, there were other sources of Energy instead of the carrot, for example qualities of the heart such as love, joy of life, wanting to make a difference or connection with others.

how to avoid
the honey traps

One of the major blocks to our spiritual development is comfort and complacency. It is the honey trap that can get us stuck just when we need some momentum to move forward. The more we are attached to our comforts, what feeds and satisfies the senses and the way we like things to be, the more change becomes difficult. Putting off the challenge for tomorrow, remaining cosseted today with friends, good food, possessions and distractions, lulls us into a false sense that we need not bother. The Buddha recounted that throughout his life the ordinary, habitual mind, which he called 'Mara', still visited him and offered him great riches were he to depart the spiritual life. Once Mara came to him with the beguiling invitation to take things easy. 'You have plenty of time to practice in the future,' it said. 'Why do you need to practice so hard? Just enjoy life like a baby at the breast'. The Buddha saw it was Mara and exclaimed: 'Just as someone whose clothes or hair had caught fire would make an extraordinary effort, and use great Mindfulness to extinguish the fire... so that person should put forth extraordinary effort, enthusiasm, Mindfulness and Wisdom to develop refined qualities'.

The tempting thoughts of comfort can continue to sap our Energy and determination all along the way. If Mara visited even the Buddha, it will certainly visit you and me. We may set up all kinds of conditions for our spiritual practice: it should be only with this teacher, when it is not too cold or hot, in comfortable accommodation, with a nice view, if the food is good, if it is not too taxing, if I have a sacred space in my house and so on. Within the experience of our practice this voice continues to entice us to replace the meditation cushion with a cushioned life. It might suggest that we can shorten our meditation time and that we practice only if the experience is pleasant and relaxing and if the insights come when I need them. We stop if the hard stuff comes up, if there is noise outside or if there are too many thoughts and noise inside.

We can also get quite complacent if we enjoy some limited benefits from inner or outer work. This is Mara tempting us with the honey trap of feel-good spirituality. Feeling good is wonderful and a natural consequence of inner development. But it can be like an energy drink, which has short term benefits but rebounds in the long term. If it becomes a place to stop, to feel good with our 'success', the journey grinds to a halt. It would be like Odysseus getting stuck in a local pub at the start of his expedition. We need to keep going, on and up, since the benefits get ever more profound as we do so.

There are several ways to deal with Mara. The first is to recognise, as the Buddha did, that this is a beguiling voice within ourselves and we must pay it no heed. If we know intimately how our feet feel when they touch the ground, we give less power to thoughts that tell us that we should turn back. We gradually learn not to give such voices authority over us. We see them as painful, debilitating and constraining mental fluff and knock them off centre stage.

Another method is to cut them dead. This is like using the sword of insight. It cuts the chains of unhelpful mental and emotional constructions there and then. It is based on an awareness that we absolutely don't need to go down that unhelpful road. It is like the shout in the Tibetan Dzogchen tradition: a sudden shout is sometimes used – Phat! – that stops the mind in its tracks and opens an empty space of awareness and freedom.

A huge amount of Energy is lost in whirlpools of the mind, which are like pressing the gas pedal in neutral gear. These leeches in the mind and heart are often about what I should be doing, what I am not doing, what is right for me, when I should do it in the future, what I need to fix within myself, what I need to get, what I should give up, what will be the best for me and who am I anyway. Much of it is based around the me and mine, which is like a huge parasitic operating system that takes up much of the space and keeps us very busy. As such it is a serious Energy sink.

We can side-line it by zooming in on the experience of the now. We refresh and reconnect ourselves with the lived moment and this meeting with life as it is renews our Energy and lightness of being. It goes along with learning to trust our first thoughts, to live in the present. This does need a bit of Wisdom to distinguish first thoughts that come as intuition and those that are driven by whims. But first thoughts are often the right ones, and if they are not, we can dare to fail or to make mistakes and not give them a second thought either. A famous Zen piece of advice sums it up: it doesn't matter so much what you do, but above all don't wobble!

from friction
to harmony

We often need friction to move forward. We could not walk without the friction between our feet and the ground. In our spiritual life, we may sometimes need resistance to develop. Think of the case where our heart feels blocked, flat or disconnected. It is sending messages, but if we don't listen it puts up a wall in the subconscious. As soon as we can let the heart sing us its song, even if it is fear, disappointment or woundedness, we will meet its resistance, break through the wall and then the heart can move. There is a beautiful line from the poet Wendell Berry: 'The impeded stream is the one that sings.'

But Energy can also be easily lost in friction, which uses up Energy and creates heat and noise. There are some basic frictions in our everyday relationships with the world, which consume Energy. Think of the amount of noise around us and the cacophony in our thoughts, or the conflict in our life: small daily irritations of neighbours, annoying arguments within the family, struggle at the workplace, even real fights that sometimes break out. There is even a basic friction in the belief in a 'me and mine' versus the world out there, as two separate entities which face off against each other. We see it in the constant busyness to control circumstances that we assume are threatening, challenging and unexpected. This uses up a huge amount of Energy in our life, Energy which could be put to much better use in expanding our consciousness and our heart. Harmony gives Energy, while friction uses it. Harmony is quiet, while friction is noisy.

For example, if we plunge into conflict with someone, watch what happens. Observe the way the verbal heat and responses arise towards the other person based on our fears and insecurities, the anger taking us over, the obsessive thinking about how to deal with that person, the strategies and fantasies and the feelings of ourselves as wronged and perhaps the victim.

Now imagine a saner and healthier alternative: from an inner place of stillness and equanimity, we track our first responses to the other person and let them go without building anything out of them. And we can be together with the other, look them in the eyes, feel where they are coming from and allow some compassionate understanding to arise in place of defensiveness. Now multiply this a thousand times to reflect all our interactions with passing circumstances in daily life. Each one can lift up the Energy of the heart, instead of draining it in constant friction. Notice that this process employs all The Five Powers in a wise and integrative way: Trust as the kinder and more harmonious outcome, Mindfulness as a significant power of transforming the situation by seeing it as it is, calmness instead of the nervous energy of conflict and Wisdom as the bigger picture of togetherness.

the antidote to discouragement

Sometimes the demands seem too great for us, the journey too long, the benefits too uncertain and we doubt our own capacity to continue. Whether it is the road to awakening, or the book we start to write, or a change we want to make in the world, it can sometimes seem endless and quite beyond us. This helplessness can sap our Energy and our will to continue. If we have that attitude, life will of course come up with confirmation. This may be in the discouraging voices of people around us or proof that we don't have what it takes and we should leave it all to better times or the next life.

One antidote to discouragement is primal joy, which always releases a surge of Energy. The path can and should bring us the joy of discovery, the joy of opening the heart and the joy of being in touch with our life as we live it. Joy is also in the now and silences the comparing mind. It comes naturally when we stop our climb for a moment. When we breathe deeply and take in the view, or get up from the computer and home in on a blackbird singing outside, or when in meditation we experience the dance of life in our cells and tissues. It is fed by moments of grace and ease and by the support of others who are with us. Gradually the joy becomes quieter, steadier and more subtle, mellowing into gladness and contentment. Those moments are precious; we can dive into them and embrace them completely and they will be with us as our magic potions for when the going gets tough.

We can also counter doubt and discouragement by looking closely at where we are right now. We can see that we are besieged by thoughts and judgements that measure ourselves and look for milestones. If we keep coming back down to where we are, the actions we are taking right now, the presence we feel in life, then we will mark the end of the tendency to measure ourselves and compare our situation to imagined goals or to others.

Once the Buddha met some Jain yogis who had been undergoing rigorous ascetic practice and intense striving for some time. The conversation went something like this: 'Why are you doing this?' 'Because we want to burn up all our negative karma and suffering to become enlightened saints'. 'So how much karma have you burnt up so far?' 'We don't know.' 'How much longer will you have to go?' 'We don't know'. 'How will you know when you have reached the goal?' 'We don't know'. 'So maybe you had better try something else – to experience your freedom in the here and now?'

how to work
with impatience

No matter how much a broody hen longs to hear her chicks cheeping and pecking at their shells, it will not happen until twenty-one days have passed. Impatience uses up Energy, makes us restless and agitated, pushes the goal further away and is rooted in the sense that we want to be somewhere other than where we are now. Ordinary practical projects and activities may lend themselves to time-based expectations, but in the field of the sublime and in authentic presence, expectations and timelines disappear. Shifts in awareness happen in their own time, often unexpectedly and – as we saw in the story of the Jains – are not in our hands to control and measure. Awakening of various kinds doesn't obey the usual human concepts of time. Impatience is our issue, but awakening is not, it is not something that we can get. It is more an awareness that we fall into while falling out of everything else.

So, we need patience as one of the expressions of refined Energy. On one level patience can sometimes feel like an annoying struggle against impatience, but on a deeper experiential level it can be a sense of stillness and quiet, like the chicken sitting on its eggs. As T. S. Eliot writes: 'I said

to my soul, be still and wait without hope for hope would be hope for the wrong thing...' Whenever impatience, goal chasing or frustration appear because we want things to move faster, we just need to use the mantra: 'what's the hurry?' If we keep letting go of the painful habit of control and expectation, patience gradually opens out into a purified state of Energy. It becomes a way of life and begins to filter into everything we do. We find ourselves talking, thinking and acting in a more measured and timeless way. The power of Energy and the power of Calm merge. You don't usually find spiritual teachers babbling away like radio talk show hosts. Their steady Energy is the same whether catching a mouse or catching a train. All of us can change our pace if we feel that the source of action comes from deep within, like our soft regular heartbeat, instead of troubled reactivity from the surface.

If we keep letting go of the painful habit of control and expectation, patience gradually opens out into a purified state of Energy

zen and
the zone

It is possible to transcend all striving, to have access to Energy that is based on stillness and connectedness with the world. If we are not trying to get anything from the world, but are simply merged with it, then no effort is needed as there is nowhere to go. This is what happens when a marathon runner breaks through the wall of resistance and finds themselves in The Zone, where running is happening by itself. It is part of the Zen practice of archery, painting and just sweeping leaves, in which there is no gap between the doer, the doing and the target or purpose. It is the result of deep meditation.

From the peak, there is nowhere else to go. If we rest there in communion with everything, the horizon, the sky and ourselves, nothing is missing and no effort is needed. Once we are there, we realise that this peak was in us from the beginning. It does not necessarily need years of onerous climbing. We take ourselves wherever we go. Indeed, whenever we arrive somewhere else beyond where or who we were, we realise that the view was with us from the beginning. It is our deeper nature that was forgotten. We can get a sense of it any time. If we stand with quiet awareness under a tree, we may feel moments of deep stillness in which there

is nothing that needs to be changed and nowhere else that is better. We can listen to the song that both the tree and ourselves are singing. A hint of perfection. It can be in mindful walking or movement, in meditation or in just simply being. The Energy of our spiritual life becomes like that of a grandfather watching the children play on the grass, a shepherdess resting in the shade watching the sheep peacefully grazing nearby.

The effort to get somewhere else implies that the place we were in was inadequate. Yet perfection cannot be over there: it is here! The start is also the end. Ultimately, the journey itself is an illusion, for there is nowhere we can get to other than where we are. This is a sublime paradox. The realisation that no effort is required and that the journey is illusion may itself require great effort to achieve. The root of the paradox lies in the insight into our true nature. If we fully grasp the big picture (that is, the big picture fully grasps us), we see how the world and ourselves make each other. This is true spirituality, unlimited, beyond the personal point of view. Then life lives itself through us and no effort is needed. We are made of, to use a Buddhist term, the Natural Great Perfection, and the way to realise this is by non-doing, 'non-meditation'. There is nothing left to do or undo, and things just happen by themselves.

The Third Power

Mindfulness

Sati

MINDFULNESS | PRESENCE | AWARENESS

how do we know we exist?

As we read this, do we know we exist? Do we know we have a body?

Of course, we know we exist! And obviously we know we have a body. But it's a fair question to ask how much, during our day-to-day life, are we truly aware that we have a body? When we walk to the car, to the shops, to a meeting – do we know we are walking? Are we aware of even one step, or is our mind full of where we are supposed to be, all that we must do and what might or might not happen?

We take thousands of breaths every single day; are we aware of any of them? Do we know we have a head? Probably not, unless we have a headache. In which case we might take a pill so we can go back to forgetting we have a head as soon as possible. We live parallel to our life but not truly in it. As John Lennon said: 'Life is what happens to you while you are busy making other plans.'

To experience life more fully, we need to practice Mindfulness. Mindfulness is being awake: aware, attentive and alert to what is really happening at this very moment. Its opposite is non-mindfulness: being asleep, distracted, switched off, running on autopilot and missing what is happening around us.

Another good word that is used to describe Mindfulness is presence. This hints at being fully there with our life in each present moment, instead of being lost in the past and writing our scripts for the future. In a deeper sense, however, Mindfulness also goes beyond the present. Real, intimate awareness with what is, is timeless. Time just isn't needed in the moment of true seeing.

An image may be helpful: our attention is a tool, like a lamp that lights up what we focus on. When we notice what we usually ignore or don't see, it is like shining a light in a dark place. We are a bit like a queen or king: our palace is the whole range of experiences of our body, mind, heart and feelings, of our surroundings and of unfolding events. But many rooms in our palace are shrouded in darkness. Mindfulness is the lamp that brings light to those empty rooms. No matter how long they have been in darkness, the lamp of our attention will light them up.

Zooming in on ordinary experiences – the sensation of our feet on the earth as we walk, the touch of the wind on our cheeks – can illuminate them, making them special, almost magical. We become fascinated by a convoy of ants carrying seeds across our path and watch them for ages. Our friends may think we have gone a bit crazy. Let them! We see the tiny plants by the roadside, unnoticed for years. This is a welcome to hidden life!

why do we keep falling into non-awareness

When we are consumed by what we have to do, what we want or don't want and what the issues are that we need to take care of, our life seems contracted. We are dedicated purely to outcomes and goals. This is forgetting, shutting down. At best, we remember in bits and pieces: as we sit by the sea or walk in the woods. Mostly, we forget.

Since these habits of forgetting are so strong, we keep falling into non-awareness. The word for Mindfulness in the ancient Pali language of the Buddhist texts is 'Sati' meaning remembering to be present, coming back into awareness. Early translators of this word into English used a rather old-fashioned English word: 'recollection'. We forget all the time. We forget to be aware because we get caught up in our interests, needs, thoughts, fantasies, and inner noise. Even though we may forget again and again, we can keep coming back, keeping our appointment with life.

Just as we wake up in the morning to the beauty of the rising sun, so can we wake up to a bigger world of experience in every

moment: our soft breath, the shapes of clouds or the depth behind the eyes of another. We just need to remember to be available.

the origin of mindfulness

Around 2600 years ago, the ex-prince Gautama became totally and irreversibly free during a momentous night of deep contemplation under the Banyan tree. He was the Buddha, which means 'the awakened one'. He tried to explain to others what happened to him, at first using high words that spoke of totality and ultimate truth. The people he met thought he had gone crazy. So, Gautama modified his teachings to address the practical issue of suffering and the cessation of suffering. What is stopping us from achieving awakening, total unconditional freedom?

In Buddhism, understanding what stops us being free is more important than theorizing about freedom. Freedom appears by itself if we remove the obstacles to it. Therefore, the teaching concentrates on the tools and methods we can use to undo the obstacles. The Buddhist texts are entirely practical guidance. That is their priceless gift to us today, a uniquely vast and deep teaching on the ways that any of us, the reader reading this and the writer writing it, can know utter and complete freedom in this life.

In the Buddhist tradition, Mindfulness is the ground of practice. The Buddha described it as the elephant's footprint, so large that it can contain the footprints of all the other animals. Mindfulness can contain all the other methods and ways of inner development. It is central to most Buddhist traditions. Indeed, in one form or another, the practice of being aware is part of all spiritual traditions. Yet the elegance, richness, depth and sophistication of this teaching in the Buddhist tradition means that we cannot seek a better authority than those texts of so long ago.

Over the years, the teachings have diverged along many paths – the Tibetan schools, Zen, the Theravada traditions of Burma, Sri Lanka, Cambodia and Thailand, Chinese Chan Buddhism and now Western versions of the teachings. However, Mindfulness has remained for all of them as one of the key practices. As spiritual practice evolves into religion over time, it becomes a social and cultural institution as well as a group identity. Over the centuries this has also happened to the Buddhist teachings, which lost their primary focus as a spiritual practice. Mindfulness and meditation were largely forgotten and even monasteries were dominated by chanting, devotion and the study of texts and codes of behaviour.

Then, in the middle of the 20th century the teachings were 'rediscovered' by a few pioneers. The West, with its interest in 'the mind' and psychology, its secularism, its belief in individual transformation and its own brand of suffering avidly took to them. Meditation and retreat centres sprang up everywhere and Mindfulness became a major practice throughout the world, as well as being reseeded in the East.

In 1976, when I came back to London after doing my first Vipassana course in India, I felt very alone as a practicing Buddhist. There was some curiosity about Buddhist practices, largely due to the books of Alan Watts and Aldous Huxley, but few practitioners and even fewer groups.

Today, you can find Mindfulness in most hospitals, many schoolrooms and in prisons. It has also entered the corporate world. An all-party committee of the British Parliament produced a major report ('Mindful Nation UK') that recommended making Mindfulness available under the NHS for patients with depression or chronic health problems. Mindfulness has also had a major influence on psychology, with Cognitive Behavioural Therapy and offshoots like Acceptance and Commitment Therapy becoming popular worldwide. Often divorced from its Buddhist roots, Mindfulness is mostly regarded as a useful technique. Nevertheless, it remains a gateway through which the profundity of Buddhist practice has entered Western society.

the promise and the proof

The first questions that naturally arise are: how can it help me? Does it really work or is it just another fad? What might I reasonably expect from it? Mindfulness is a way to turn towards the issues that trouble us, seeing them as experiences we can work with, rather than problems. There is no doubt that regarding our issues more wisely, freely, clearly and kindly can make a big difference. There are literally thousands of scientific research publications on Mindfulness showing a wide variety of very practical benefits for specific mind-body problems. Of the many examples, one we might consider first is stress. How are we when we feel under great pressure – the agitation, the Sisyphean sense of endless work, the tension in the stomach? We can watch these signs with a detached, interested clarity, as if they don't belong to us. Calmness will arrive and in the long term, more health. There is a great deal of evidence that Mindfulness can bring improved well-being, effectiveness and even ethical sensitivity to the staff of corporations and organisations. Mindfulness works with children. Few of us would envy teachers trying to control and teach unruly, agitated and noisy classes. But when children have classes of Mindfulness, in which they sit or lie down and return to themselves and reconnect with their own minds and hearts, many reports show major improvements in attention and learning, calmness and reduced stress.

Mindfulness can help us to step out of and not be submerged in, many mild psychological disturbances. Consider the many reports that Mindfulness is at least as good and often better than other psychiatric and psychological interventions in anxiety and mild depression and lasts longer. Equally, consider chronic pain. Pain clinics throughout the world have found that when all else fails, Mindfulness can bring more well-being, better pain management and less medication. The pain may still there, but the suffering is reduced. Or imagine poor and disturbed sleep, spending night after night tossing and turning. Mindfulness can kick in instead, bringing the attention to heaviness and relaxation in the body and the gentle rhythm of the breath in the belly, inviting sleep. Even in serious diseases, such as cancer, there is now a great deal of evidence of improvements in physical and mental health status, immune capacity and many other health indications.

Mindfulness in the ancient Pali language of the Buddhist texts is Sati, meaning remembering to be present

can mindfulness
make us better people?

A fundamental axiom of the spiritual journey is that it must be based on some degree of inner goodness and moral sensitivity. If Mindfulness is merely a technique, it could, for instance, be used by a burglar to be more effective at quietly burgling a house. Has modern-day Mindfulness abandoned the ethical ground from which it grows? This can be a concern, but when we look at the big picture with more compassion, we can see that modern Mindfulness can be an aid to developing moral sensibility. The major source of harmful and unethical action is not an evil heart but a blocked, self-interested perception that is blind to the consequences of our actions. As Saint Bernard of Clairvaux told us, the road to hell is paved with good intentions.

Mindfulness has the power to encourage us to be more empathic, watchful and aware, more alert to what we do and how we act and to the consequences of our actions. A personal example: I have a vegetable garden, which I tend carefully. It provides a good deal of the vegetables we consume in our home. Many is the time that visitors, full of ecological enthusiasm and eagerness to help, have arrived and marched straight into the middle of the vegetable garden. They don't notice that they are trampling cabbage seedlings underfoot! Here, Mindfulness would serve them better than good intentions. The documentary 'Doing Time, Doing Vipassana' records a ten-day Mindfulness meditation retreat attended by prisoners in an Indian jail. The prisoners emerge from the retreat with tears in their eyes, embracing their jailers, who are also moved to tears by the depth of the experience. The prisoners explain in the documentary that the self-awareness they had practised showed them their responsibility for their own actions. Instead of blaming others, they recognized the part they played and the harm they caused. Mindfulness is fundamentally an ethical act: we can take responsibility for our actions if we notice how and why we do them and if they are helpful or harmful.

There are many reasons we may decide to practice Mindfulness. We may have heard about it from friends and believe that it will help us: we want to be calmer, more centred, clearer about our choices, less depressed or anxious and so on. These reasons prompt us to start the journey up the mountain. There is something to be done, a mission to be accomplished. Without such motivation, we wouldn't even start the journey. But the motivation is a double-edged sword. It can lead to pressure that experiences on the way should live up to expectations that might be unrealistic, are certainly not reliable and can lead to a constant measuring of how far we have come and how far there is still to go. This judging, measuring and comparing takes us out of Mindfulness, not into it.

Mindfulness is about the flow of direct experiences in the present moment. If we assume that Mindfulness should help us to be calm, yet our mind seems to be a shouting babble, we can easily become disheartened and give up. We forget that we are doing it correctly, otherwise we would not even be able to see what is going on in our minds. To enter the practice of Mindfulness, we need to let go of all expectations and wisely, patiently, calmly listen to the voices of our mind and body and the world. The climb becomes a stroll.

At the bottom of the mountain, we may be concerned with handling stress. As we ascend, we may realise that the stress is caused by psychological patterns of insecurity and in fact this is what we want to dissolve. As we go higher still, we see that the insecurity is the result of deep unconscious conditioning and old wounds and our motivation is to clean and dissolve those fixations. As we continue, the motivation becomes more and more subtle. We may be inspired by the wish to explore, by the sense of discovery in the new powers and capacities within us and of inner development. Yet further up the path, the longing becomes more spiritual, a quest for deep meaning. As we approach the summit, there is no need for motivation: the path carries us onwards and then disappears. There is nowhere left to go except the ever-present now.

The early texts clearly describe how to practice Mindfulness. Start by sitting quietly and as the text says, 'let go of concerns and worries about the world'. Then, when breathing in a long breath

you know it is a long breath, when breathing a short breath you know it is a short breath... when stretching out the arm you know it, when turning, walking, sitting, eating – you know it... and so on. You know sounds and tastes, touch and smells.

That is on the level of body. It gets subtler, of course. When a thought arises, you know that you are thinking and you know what kind of thought it is. You know when you are attracted

or pulled towards something you like or pushed away from something you don't like. You know the arising of intentions and will, of moods and states of mind. You know the inner emotional climate, subtle or gross forms of anger, joy, love and every other feeling. You know what it's like to be you at every moment. In this present moment we experience a flow of ever-changing impressions and experiences. Getting closer to this truth we begin to feel fully and wonderfully alive, much as we did when we were children.

Mindfulness can be practiced in any position If we are sitting on a chair, it is helpful to have both feet touching the floor side by side and to sit erect but without strain – like a pharaoh. If on the floor, our legs can be crossed or in any position, but it is helpful to raise our buttocks by sitting on a cushion so as to bring our knees closer to the floor and sit erect, not collapsing, but comfortable.

But we do not have to sit. We can stand too – or walk or lie down. Each position has a slightly different character and effect and the objects of Mindfulness might be slightly different, which we will discuss below. If standing, we stand relaxed but tall, steady and rooted into the earth like an oak tree. The knees can be very slightly bent instead of locked. If walking, we walk very slowly, one step at a time, with our eyes gently focused in front, like a bride walking up the aisle. If lying, we can lie on one side, reclining, or flat on our back with hands to the side in the yogic 'corpse' pose.

Mindfulness is about coming home, back to ourselves, from a scattered, stressed, busy, fragmented and disconnected daily life. We can begin by gathering ourselves together. We might sense the body in a general way and become aware of sounds – the birds or the traffic outside.

We wind down and come to a halt, like a train arriving at its terminus. This can be a most enjoyable and delightful stopping, a stepping out of the race and of the habitual need to be doing something. This attitude is more like a deep rest that we deserve, a gift that we give to ourselves, rather than another project that we need to do because it is good for us. If we are going to make this practice part of our daily life, it needs to be as natural, easy and joyful as a walk in the garden or relaxing in our favourite armchair and not another chore on our to-do list, otherwise we will soon give it up.

Mindfulness is the flow of direct experiences in the present moment

the place to begin:
have the body in mind

Thoughts and impressions come marching in, as is their habit. They will tend to sweep us away from presence into their stories. We forget. At that point we can give priority to bodily experience. Focus on some clear aspect of bodily life: if sitting, focus on the touch of the hands or the experience of pressure on the buttocks; if standing and walking, focus on the feet or the general flow of bodily sensations in various part of the body. We can spend some time in quiet and steady focus on 'the bodiness of the body', in the words of the Buddhist text. We may just rest in the sense that 'there is a body'. Or from here we may actually check in to various parts of the body and listen to what each part is telling us: whether it is comfort or discomfort, ease or stress and contraction, subtle sensations or gross ones, heat or cold, the touch of the clothes. Whatever we notice.

One Cambodian Buddhist monk I knew, who was at least 100 years old when I met him, said that his daily morning practice was to move over the body, part-by-part, conversing with each part: 'Right ear, how are you? I am happy. Good. Left ear, how are you? I am happy. Good. ...Upper lip, how are you...'

At the centre of our being is the breath. The breath is the primary address for our Mindfulness practice. It is subtle, therefore invites us in under the surface. It is rhythmical, inviting us to feel carried by its waves into a Calm space. It is precious and important as the breath of life. It connects between inside and outside, as each breath brings into our being the outbreath of the forests, the seas and we return the breath to the endless world. It is interesting, since each breath is different and shows us something about ourselves – whether we are open or contracted, tense or relaxed, insecure or at ease. The breath is also a bridge between mind and body, partly in our control and partly uncontrolled, showing us both aspects if we are watching.

Home in on the in-breath and out-breath, wherever they are clearest, which is often in the rising and falling of the belly but could also be the chest or nostrils. Is it smooth or rough, is it flowing or contracted, is it controlled or free, is it associated with any feelings or responses?

Let intimacy with the breath take us to a place of quiet, steady presence. Let go into it. Let the breath breathe us. It is a ground or anchor that will help us maintain mindful awareness. Even when thoughts take us away again and again, the breath leads us back home. It can also help change mood and feelings. As we breathe out, we can let go and release all the tensions, issues and subtle places of stress. As we breathe in, we can feel energised and 'inspired' (from the Latin inspirare, meaning in-breath). Sometimes we can let the breath be an internal massage that softens and soothes places of stress and discomfort in our body and mind.

mindfulness requires investigation

Ninety percent of an iceberg is under the surface and invisible. Ninety percent of our brain is unused. Mindfulness expands our power to see under the surface, to bring into awareness what is usually invisible and unknown. The world gets bigger and we emerge from the tunnel vision which has restricted our life and our possibilities. We see more, know more, live more and feel more. For example, we can easily become much more creative and adventurous in our life. Doors open that we didn't know existed.

There is a Sufi tale of a man who found himself in prison. He sent a message to his friends outside to send him some tools, a hammer, a screwdriver, even a gun, with which he could smash the lock on the door and escape. Eventually a parcel came and with great enthusiasm and expectation he tore it open. Imagine

his disappointment when he realised that all there was inside was a prayer carpet. He threw it in the corner and sulked. After a couple of weeks, he decided he might as well use the carpet, and began to pray on it, five times a day. After another couple of weeks, in the middle of his prayers, with his nose close to the carpet, he became aware that the pattern in the carpet was complex and interesting. On closer examination he suddenly realised that the pattern woven into the carpet was the design of the lock. With this knowledge he was able to open the lock and walk free.

Mindfulness requires investigation. It invites us to go beyond superficial first impressions to deeply explore and penetrate our experience. See everything in a higher resolution: when walking, break it up into steps, a step into touching the ground with each foot, the changes in the weight and pressure. What is really going on? What is one step really like?

When we listen to the voices of body and mind, like a mother to a child, we are also using the power of the heart. It is built into the practice, for how could such closeness and intimacy with our

life and the lives of others create unkindness or alienation? To use the example of our eyes, if we relax and bathe our eyes with attention and care, we are giving them love. When we connect with our real life, we support it, even if we do not know that we do so. Mindfulness is always kind. It invites in any guest, however troublesome, for tea.

Here is where the power of Trust and that of Mindfulness go hand in hand. When we turn to something that annoys us, such as the pain in the back or the irritating voice of our neighbour and look at it directly with interest and deep listening, we join it, instead of fighting it or wanting it to disappear. Our heart opens to it as we see the life in it.

We see more, know more, live more
and feel more

looking at ourselves with kind eyes

We can be purposeful and actually empower the kind heart during practice. We do this by introducing softness into our power of attention. When we pay attention to an immediate experience, such as the way the body feels at any given moment, or a place of stress or tension, we actively turn towards it with an attitude of support. We are consciously for it, not against it. We embrace it like a mother holding a child and know that our attention itself is like mother's milk.

Kindness can be applied to all experiences, whatever they are. We often give ourselves a hard time, and we have a tendency, especially in the modern world, to constantly run the voices of criticism and judgement of ourselves and others in the background. We assume these voices to be true: things are not good enough, we are not good enough, the world is all wrong and needs fixing and more, that we ourselves need fixing. Mindfulness can reveal these thoughts as thoughts and not reality, and even note them as: 'judgemental thought'. Trust can change our attitude to them, beaming friendliness to ourselves and also to the thoughts, instead of being judgemental about being judgemental. It is as if we are saying to them: 'I hear you, it's OK.'

William Blake tells us that 'Man was made for joy and woe; And when this we rightly know. Through the world we safely go.' Things happen, events transpire, experiences arise. Some are pleasant, some unpleasant. The body might hurt a bit or feel warm and very pleasant. There may be uncomfortable thoughts – anxious, obsessive, shaming or blaming, but we do not need to censor the unpleasant and hunt for the pleasant. What comes through the senses and mind is the raw material. We invite it in.

One of the extraordinary benefits of Mindfulness is that it teaches us to accept the rose's thorns as well as its petals. It is a way of seeing that does not give preference to what I want or what I don't want. Shakespeare said: 'there is nothing either good or bad but thinking makes it so'.

As Rumi writes:

Being human is like a guest house
Each morning a new arrival.
A joy, a depression, a bad mood
Comes as an unexpected visitor.
Welcome and entertain them all!
Meet them at the door laughing,
And invite them in.
Be grateful for whoever comes,
Because each has been sent
As a guide from beyond.

If we can invite in both pain and pleasure for a cup of tea, if we can hold both with attention and care, if we can be equally ready to allow the crying baby and the laughing one, we find extraordinary freedom. We are not swept away by our needs, aversions, resistances and desires, but find ourselves steady, independent and free. We become something greater than the sum of our conflicting states.

There will always be feelings of pain and pleasure. We need them. Pain tells us there is something to be done, hunger tells us we need to eat. But we do not need to build worlds of stories, narratives, issues, habits, reactivity and protective walls from such sensory inputs.

A famous Buddhist parable expresses this well. It is called the Second Arrow. A man is struck by an arrow. It causes pain but then comes loose and drops down. Instead of leaving it there, the man picks it up and continues stabbing himself with it: 'Why me?' 'It always happens to me.' 'I am sure it came from them; I will have revenge!' 'I will never get over it.' 'I am so depressed.' 'I will never forget this insult.' 'This is a miserable life.'

difficult
visitors

Unwelcome guests often take the form of mind-body states that make us uncomfortable and distracted. In the traditional formulation there are five of them.

First, desire, neediness, wanting something other than what we experience at this moment. It could be the urgent need for a cup of coffee, a look at WhatsApp, the news, more money, seeing someone close to us, new clothes. The possibilities are endless.

Second, aversion and resistance. This may be to external disturbances such as the neighbour's television or kids, or a discomfort in the body, or to doing Mindfulness, or to someone you know, or to bacteria, or to memories, or to the place you sit in, or to the weather, or to the politicians... the targets are endless.

Third, restlessness. You feel you need to move all the time; the thoughts keep disturbing at a furious pace, the body is restless and can't settle, you want to run away but don't know to where, the to-do list seems critical.

Fourth, lack of Energy, drowsiness, switching off. Every time we practice our head drops and we fall into a half sleep, a vague hypnotic state, or a dream or sense of overwhelming tiredness, we want to keel over, or we feel dull, heavy, blank. Fifth, confusion, doubt, endless uncertainty, running commentary, a paralytic muddle.

The key is a 180-degree shift in our attitude to these guests that come barging in and upsetting the furniture. They are not problems that block Mindfulness, they are the invitations to Mindfulness. They are teachers, not nuisances, because they show us the edge or the limits where we need to practice. They are like the "X' on the treasure map that says: dig here. In order to work with these apparent obstacles, think RAIN:

R. Recognise these guests as unwanted but important phenomena. What does this guest look like? Which of the above five does it belong to? What is it doing to me?

A. Accept the actual experience of this phenomenon as it is. Allow may even be a better word; allowing it to be what it is even if not so pleasant or comfortable. We are with it, not against it, it is a partner, not an enemy.

I. Investigate its nature. Intimacy may be an even better word. What is the actual experience? Where exactly do I feel it? In the body, mind or feelings? How is it moving, changing, strengthening, weakening and altering its appearance? What am I doing with it – what are my reactions, responses, narratives, comments and projections around it?

N. Non-identification is our ability to step out of it, to see it as a guest and not as us, to hold it in awareness but not to let it take us over, seeing it just as a phenomenon. This last step purifies us from it, weakening it and cleaning our conscious and unconscious

mind from these patterns, habits and tendencies. This last step is crucial – it is our path to deep and lasting freedom and well-being.

feelings and emotions

We are often overwhelmed by anger, sadness, anxiety, fear, frustration, shame or guilt and also by positive emotions of enthusiasm, joy, power, love and laughter. We mostly long to be free of the control of the negative emotions, which can take us into destructive, painful and unhelpful places. We keep trying to enhance the positive emotions and develop them, despite the sometimes unkind conditions of daily life. Mindfulness of emotional life helps us to experience emotions as partners and a source of Energy and life, rather than as controlling dictators.

We often think that emotions should be suppressed ('stiff upper lip') or expressed ('don't hold it in'). But there is a huge territory between suppression and expression and that is our capacity to fully experience our emotional life, meeting it head-on, with steadiness and emotional intelligence.

When strong emotions arise, we can take a breath or two in order to gather ourselves and then see the way the emotion expresses itself in our bodies and in our hearts. Where is it mostly in the body? What are the thoughts that go with it? Is it pleasant or unpleasant? What kind of emotion is it? How is it developing and changing? If someone says something rude and hurtful, see the way the words impact, see what button in us has been pressed, see the rise of reactivity and feeling, see the painful power of the emotion and then see the way it naturally dies away.

Sometimes, as in the case of fear, emotions seem to be so overwhelming that they carry us away and are unavailable to Mindfulness. It is usually because they recruit all of us: bodily symptoms, mental stories, hormonal changes, unconscious habits, painful memories, the lot. Therefore, we need to cut them down to size, get a handle on them. Try choosing just one place in the body, such as the contracted belly, to track the changes during an emotional episode. It is as if we press the 'minimise screen' button on the computer and a whole program collapses into a small icon, which is much easier to hold with Mindfulness.

One of the extraordinary benefits of Mindfulness is that it teaches us to accept the rose's thorns as well as its petals

anger isn't yours

There is a Zen story about a student that came to his Zen teacher and said: 'Master, please help me deal with my anger.' 'Sure,' said the teacher, 'Bring me the anger and we will deal with it together.' 'But right now, I don't have it,' said the student. 'OK, so when anger arises next time, bring it and we will deal with it together,' answered the teacher. 'But Master,' complained the student, 'it will take me 10 minutes to get from my room to yours and in that time the anger will surely have gone.' 'You see,' answered the teacher, 'anger comes and goes when it wants not when you want. Even if you want anger you can't get it. It belongs to the Universe, not to you. That's how to deal with anger!'

I remember that I had a very specific but devastating problem when I was teaching at Chelsea College, London University, in the late 1970s. It was fear of public speaking. Every time I needed to give a lecture I was in a panic. As soon as I went up onto the stage, my mouth went dry, my stomach contracted, my heart raced, sweat poured down and I wanted the earth to swallow me up.

Fortunately, I had already been practicing Mindfulness in some retreats and I was determined to use it for solving the problem. So, during retreats I imagined myself in front of students and when the signs of fear arose, I just helped them directly with awareness, exploring them as they were in the body and mind – seeing how they arrived and departed. In addition, I started coming in a couple of minutes early before each lecture. As the students filed in, the signs of fear would arise automatically. But I would take just one symptom – usually contraction of the stomach and just turn my attention to it as a phenomenon of no importance. Gradually this fear left me and though it took around a year to dissolve, I have no trace of it left.

the power to rewrite
our narratives

Another short personal story to illustrate this approach. One time I was approached by a young mother. She was thin, wiry, with sharp piercing eyes. She had Wisdom behind those eyes, but she seemed a bit like a fugitive, agitated. She told me that her son was autistic and went to a special school. He was, to her, an amazing boy who gave her a lot of delight. But she felt a great deal of pain from her daily struggles to take care of him and particularly from her identification with the boy's suffering. She was longing to escape somewhere, to find silence, peace and withdraw into a cave.

I suggested to her that the distressing narratives concerning the pain had taken up residence in her mind and heart, leaving no room for joy and inner peace. She couldn't find her refuge because she kept skipping over it. Mindfulness would allow her to know pain directly as it is, when it arises and when goes, then to know the joy and the peace that arise in its place. This would also give her the power to rewrite the narratives, to feel appreciation instead of worry, for example for the special qualities of her son and how much he was cared for at his special school.

We may be quite engaged with Mindfulness or other spiritual practice and feel quite present in the midst of our daily life. Yet

something always seems to disturb us. 'The neighbour's TV is just such a headache. It stops me meditating'. 'I need to get away from this crazy city and go to the countryside where it is quiet, or better still to a Monastery (or a beach) in Thailand'. It never stops. I participated in one retreat in which there was a bulldozer working directly outside the hall, making a huge noise, rattling the windows and shaking the building. Someone asked the Tibetan Lama who was teaching; 'The Buddha said that you can become awakened just by the rustling of leaves. Can you also get awakened from the roar of a bulldozer?' The teacher thought for a moment, and then said: 'I have to say, yes.'

Here is a reflection: we are disturbed because we have defined a sensory stimulation as disturbing. A bulldozer, yes, birdsong, no. So, the disturbance is not in the noise but in the way we perceive it. The noise is just sound waves doing nothing. We disturbed ourselves and the noise! If we awaken to the simple experience of sensory life, to phenomenon arising and passing, we will be less vulnerable to disturbance and more equanimous.

how to meet our minds

Watch thoughts as stories that rapidly move and change. Don't believe in them or identify with them but see them as pictures that arise and pass. If you can, also sense the background consciousness out of which thoughts arise and into which they dissolve again, like waves on the ocean. This can be tricky as the thoughts are fast and they seem to be true. But if we can step out or step back from them, we can see what they say, like watching a scene in a movie. We can even give them a label. For example, the thought arises: 'Again I made the same mistake'. We can make a mental note: judgmental thought. 'I can't manage this': judgmental thought.

'Tomorrow I have to go to fix the car': planning thought. etc. This practice not only illuminates what is going on in our minds, but gradually changes our relationship to thinking, turning it more into partner, than lord and master.

My daughter is a CBT therapist who sees a lot of clients with Obsessive Compulsive Disorder, obsessive thoughts that lead to obsessive behaviours such as washing hands repeatedly throughout the day because of fear of bacteria. She helps clients to mindfully become aware of the fears, urges and thoughts just as they are: fears and thoughts, without any need to believe them or do anything with them. Her clients come to realize that their behaviour is due to a loop in their own minds, not an external reality.

We do not need to fight great heroic battles to get rid of things that bother us. We just need to notice carefully that they always go by themselves. They usually come back – psychological habits die hard – but each time we see them for what they are, rather than the demons we turn them into and see that they have a very short shelf life, they lose some of their power over us.

Mindfulness is not rumination or introspection, sucking us into endless loops in the mind. In contrast, it gives us a way to change a destructive habit, behaviour or addiction, by seeing it and its roots. Instead of being entirely caught up and enthralled by our mental movie, as if we are the leading actor in it, we can look at it with the eye of a director – the angle, the camera shot, the way

a scene is constructed. We can take responsibility for our own minds by seeing what is there, letting go of what is unhelpful and encouraging what is helpful and healthy. Slowly the cacophony in our minds is quietened and we find that it is actually our music.

mindfulness and the other powers

Mindfulness is the pathfinder among The Five Powers; it discovers the territory, views the landscape and notices what is needed. Trust and radical acceptance allow experiences that arise to be seen just as they are without barriers of rejection and resistance. A balanced Energy is needed to keep going as we engage with our inner life, neither collapsing nor exhausting ourselves with heroic ambitions. Calmness and concentration go hand in hand with Mindfulness, allowing us to stay focussed and close to what we observe so that we can watch it unfold. And Wisdom permits the liberating insights and truths that are discovered along the way.

how to live a mindful life

Exploring the subtle hidden places of our experience, such as the whole journey of one breath, requires focus and stillness and is most suitably done during a quiet period of sitting. But what about daily life? When we get up from quiet sitting, do we have to plunge back into the whirlpool of forgetfulness and busyness until the next time? Not at all.

In the context of daily life, Mindfulness is being awake. Instead of being on automatic pilot or thinking of what we need to do, pay attention to the experience of walking when we walk, of talking when we talk, of the movement of the hand as we pay for something and the eyes of the person we pay, of the dog passing by and the little flowers that grow by the side of the pavement.

In the evening, when we lie down, practice going through the body, from the head down to the toes. Check in with each part: how it feels, what are the living sensations there and how the experience is changing constantly. For example, what is the real experience of the eyes: perhaps the tiredness of their muscles, or the movement of the eyelids? Let go of interest in the mind and its disturbing chatter. Instead, drop into the body and let the body drop down into the earth. Let go of ourselves, we have no role to play. This will ensure a deep and restful sleep.

When swimming, dancing, moving, loving or just sitting, be fully aware of just that. The touch of the water, the touch of the ground, the movement of our limbs, the messages from our senses and our genuine life experience as it is really lived, known directly, without commentary, in the present moment.

healing the scars of life

Everything that we have been through is engraved somewhere in our body, in our minds and in our soul. We are dropped into a body which develops and changes dynamically according to conditions. We arrive in each moment as we are, shaped and constructed by life, bearing our history and memory, just like a tree that expresses on its trunk everything that has happened to it. And as the tree does not have a problem with the way it is shaped by life, there is no reason why we should have a problem with our shape. We can meet our history and our memory, including all the scars and wounds, whenever they arise in the present, with interest, appreciation and awareness. A difficult memory can emerge and we can feel the pain associated with it, just as a beautiful memory can emerge and we feel its joy and we may respond with tears or laughter. But then it is gone. As we develop Mindfulness we become more of a witness to what surfaces from our past and less of a victim. Stories are just stories, narratives are just narratives and embodiment is just embodiment. If we let go into this flow of life, the wounds will dissolve and the scars will be softened and brought back into circulation. We don't need to work hard to get rid of our painful patterns, memories, issues and habits. When we see them clearly, we realise that they are dynamic and come and go by themselves. We just need to let them go.

In the long term, living a mindful life can have a profound effect on our whole personality and what happens in our life. This is because who we are is based on our moment by moment awareness and if this changes, we change. Whenever we experience something, whether a beautiful flower or an unpleasant back pain, it starts somewhere deep as a primal awareness, a basic undefined trigger. Very quickly, it takes shape according to our habits, likes and dislikes, feelings, memories, conditioning and responses. Perceptions arise and then conceptions. These engrave

further habits and memories, which shape our future experiences similarly. All this shaping of experience, the constructions which we make, we think of as real. We become them.

The way we navigate through life is guided by who we assume we are and what we pay attention to. This is well-expressed in a traditional poem:

Sow a thought, reap a word.
Sow a word, reap an action.
Sow an action, reap a habit.
Sow a habit, reap a personality.
Sow a personality, reap a fate.

If we are running on automatic, we will just feel helplessly swept along by life and subject to our fate. But living with awareness will allow us to take responsibility for the way we see ourselves and transform the way we are in the world.

On a deep level, Mindfulness can also look back down the chain and meet the very source of our experience, the primal consciousness that is the empty womb that gives birth to all the forms. It is the act of knowing itself, which is prior to the known.

changing water into wine

Mindfulness in its full, original and sublime sense is a tool we can use for spiritual realisation and deep liberation. The ordinary becomes extraordinary. Water changes into wine. We lose the conventional consensus view, along with its descriptions, labels and fixations. The ordinary – the cup on our table, the fruit in the bowl, the shape of our hand and the body language of a friend – all seem more magical and original. This has profound consequences for our daily life experience. It will affect everything. We live more lightly and playfully and dance with whatever arises.

Another way of describing this is the sense of spaciousness. We feel that things have more room, are more spacious and open and less contracted. This spaciousness can expand beyond boundaries and objects, into a place that feels limitless, unbounded. This has been checked scientifically – on myself! It may not be as esoteric as it sounds. As we expand our awareness to embrace more and more of our changing experiences, we notice more and become a bigger container that easily holds whatever life throws into us. The issues that arise, whether difficult for us or pleasant, occupy less mental territory and there is more space left over for intuition, insight and an expanded consciousness. If we put a spoonful of salt into a cup of water, the water tastes very salty. But if the salt is thrown into a lake, it won't make any difference. Spiritually, the recognition of a free and spacious awareness is a major discovery concerning our true nature. 'I could be bounded in a nutshell and count myself a king of infinite space' says Hamlet.

so, what do we see when we get to the top of the mountain?

The view of course. But not just to the next mountain. It is a view that is vast and inclusive. It includes the seer, the seen and the seeing and unfolds beyond these to encompass a view of reality which is total, timeless and immeasurable. You could call it the divine or the ultimate view. Mindfulness, in the end, takes us there. And it is not just the grandeur of a mountain: it is the way we might look at a cup, or our bodies, or the moon. Can we see what connects us and the moon, not just the moon itself? Can we look at a cup with an unconditioned view and know it, not as the commonplace object that our mind has learnt to recognise and label, but a collection of all the many elements, substances and efforts that are needed to create 'cupness' in this moment? Can we see ourselves as life that is not ours but belongs to the universe?

The truth that you find at the top of the mountain is the truth you brought up with you in the first place. We have this truth within us to begin with. Without it, experiences of the sacred would be impossible. But this sacred view is obscured by layers of concepts, beliefs, interpretations, descriptions, facts, psychological and emotional patterns, memories and so forth. When we discard them by the wayside and they are washed away by the R.A.I.N. (see above), there is left pure seeing and pure being, which is limitless and in which we and the world are merged.

The Fourth Power

Calm

Samadhi

CALM | SERENITY | CONCENTRATION

Calm, concentration, steadiness and serenity combine as a power that is needed for a joyful and peaceful life. The power of Calm also complements and amplifies the other Five Powers: Trust won't work well if we are agitated in the face of any sudden change, unable to stay steady with both feet firmly placed on the ground. Mindfulness is limited if we are constantly distracted and disturbed. Energy can be used up by over-activity and stress. Wisdom requires calmness to look deeply and quietly into the life of things.

Inner quiet is always available. We can learn on the one hand how to let go of the noise and on the other hand to enjoy the silence, which also reveals those hidden voices that we usually cannot hear. This chapter explores how to develop and enjoy the power of Calm without having to run away to a forest or mountain top.

how do we learn to stop?

There is something relentless about human activity. Watching King's Cross, Grand Central, or Bombay main railway stations during rush hour reveals an extraordinary human agitation, like a disturbed beehive. But we are not the onlookers: we are part of the picture. This is not just a problem of today's world, though it is more acute now. Some two thousand years ago Plautus wrote: 'Let the Gods curse the man who first found out how to measure hours ... To cut and hack my days so wretchedly into small pieces. 'Life can feel so fast, busy, stressful and burdensome. We don't know what real peace would feel like. We keep dreaming of stopping this race by changing something in our life. If you ask people what conditions would help them to feel relaxed, contented and at peace, you would probably get responses like: 'When I laze by the sea', 'When I am walking in the forest', 'When I curl up with a good book', 'When gardening', 'When breastfeeding my new-born' and so on. We do indeed feel good in those peaceful conditions, but they seem to end too quickly. And sometimes those peaceful environments don't quite work out as we imagined they would: we go on holiday with the family and after hours stuck in traffic, we finally arrive only for everyone to bicker about what we should do next.

Doing nothing is hard and even scary. Standing still often needs more determination and purpose than just keeping going with the same habitual momentum of ceaseless activity. Research at Virginia and Harvard Universities showed that students preferred unpleasant electrical shocks to being forced to do absolutely nothing for fifteen minutes. Restless activity is a deeply ingrained personal and social habit.

We may feel quite overwhelmed or stressed out, but still driven to seek diversion and distraction. Even if we get to that cave or desert island we dreamed about, we may soon feel bored, anxious and restless again: what's in the news; can we afford this break; is our family safe and sound without us? But stopping, 'getting off the wheel', is crucial if we want to change ourselves and our world.

understanding our restless energy

From a Buddhist perspective, many kinds of running are running away, attempts to escape from unconscious existential dissatisfaction. This may be fear of being empty, of being nobody, of failure, or of uncertainty or not-knowing.

Part of restlessness is being constantly watchful of imagined threats and problems lurking behind our backs. Tigger demonstrates this universal tendency when invited to tea by Pooh. Asked to explain why he suddenly ripped the tablecloth from the table and got himself entangled in it; Tigger explains that it was trying to bite him when he wasn't looking.

One of the most famous discourses of the Buddha – so dramatic and powerful that, according to legend, a thousand people were instantly enlightened just by hearing it – is the Fire Sermon. The Buddha declaimed that once born, our senses are besieged by inputs, which trigger ceaseless desires, neediness, aversion, control, struggle and restless seeking of gratification. We are burning up, he said. His message remains contemporary two and a half millennia later: we are still on fire, with a culture built on this restless energy of over-activity, consuming, going where and when we want and burning up huge amounts of energy in the process. Our planet too is burning as a result. This furious activity is founded on a corruption of the basic human drive for survival: the need for nutrition, for example, becomes an endless drive for more choices, restaurants, interesting meals, TV chefs, shopping, products, temptations, snacks and on and on... in which we are never quite satisfied.

If we get up in the morning with a clear voice that says *enough*, we should act on it. We may need to go away, to shut up shop, for the habits of constant doing may be so strong that we need a radical change in our circumstances to make a dent in them. This is the time to go either to a retreat centre, or the forest, to sit by the sea and look at the horizon rather than the screen of a device, or to go to where we are warmed by the sun and blessed by the stars. It might even be enough to go up to that room in the attic

Life can feel so fast, busy, stressful and burdensome. We don't know what real peace would feel like.

and shut the door. Changing external conditions in such ways is not a permanent solution to a lack of inner peace, but sometimes a sticking plaster is exactly what we need.

More common ways of chilling out often provide a temporary antidote to the pressure: going to the pub, watching TV, grabbing a whisky or a joint, or trying to silence the sources of disturbance. But escape behaviours are not a viable option in the long run. Instead, finding some seclusion or solitude externally can be a vital first step to finding seclusion internally. Going off for a few days yoga or a meditation retreat, or to a cottage by the sea can be a springboard to a more permanent inner quiet. This is not 'retreat', or withdrawal as if defeated. We can look at it as progress. The Buddha's description for moving from a busy daily life to a life of seclusion and meditating under the trees, was 'going forward'.

But a word of warning: we need to treat our dependencies on busyness with a great deal of respect and attention. They are very powerful. Our hectic life is highly addictive. It is all too easy to intend not to look at our smartphone every few minutes, but our mind has other ideas. You can't stop quickly. Once, I taught a Mindfulness course for the staff at a college and as each class began the dean would be busy checking the clock, chasing latecomers and locking and unlocking the door. I joked with him that he was running in order to stop.

It takes a gradual slowing down to bring a great ship to stop and we should be careful that we don't, like the Titanic, crash and sink, be it into depression, anaesthesia or drugs. We must be kind and patient with our habits of restless activity and be realistic. Change will happen, but it needs forbearance. Other powers will help here synergistically, particularly the gift of a balanced and refined Energy and the Mindfulness to see the changes as they happen. It will take us some time and practice to beat the stillness marathons of my cat, who can sit unmoving on a carpet for hours, then stretch, yawn and settle in again for another long session of non-doing.

Stopping should not itself become a source of stress. The power of Trust will help us appreciate ourselves for making the change and responding to what was needed and we must slow down naturally, landing softly in another way of being. So, if we are up in the hills and can't help checking e-mails, we can do so without blame.

However, we may sometimes find that what we need is to grit our teeth and go through the withdrawal symptoms. If we are on our own or in silence on a retreat, the shift to solitude may spill over into a painful loneliness. Yet it may be crucial to go through that experience of solitude to the other side, rather than give in to our craving for diversion and leave. The same goes for quiet: we may need the power of determined energy to work in tandem with The power of Calm and concentration, to meet and transform the unpleasant resistance and agitation that comes up. More on that below.

how to
fix our brakes

If the whole world around is stampeding like a herd of bison, can we come to our senses, step aside and let the herd rush on without us? It is well worth looking at daily life: to what extent are we influenced by our society, environment and surroundings, and what can we let go of? Can we reduce our profile, simplify things and consciously decide not to keep up with the herd? Can we restrict the need to check messages, WhatsApp and e-mails to certain times during the day only? Can we take mini breaks during the day to do a reset?

I once taught a group of family doctors a weekly course in meditation. What really helped them to deal with the endless stream of patients was the advice to just put their hands on the table for a moment, feel the touch of the fingers, take two or three breaths and then invite the next patient in. A small shift in our daily life now can make a huge difference downstream. We should never underestimate the simple benefit of taking a walk in the park, sipping a cup of tea on the veranda, or quietly baking bread in the early morning to the applause of the birds outside.

Culture is a powerful conditioning force to encourage or discourage frenetic activity. I once taught Mindfulness to the staff of a mental hospital. There were several Arab male nurses there who really got it – they had an impressive natural ability to embrace deep silence in our sessions. I asked them how they did it. One of them said: 'We have it in our culture. When we come home from work, we sit on our veranda with a water pipe for an hour or two, just relaxing. What you are teaching us to do is to sit smoking the water pipe without the water pipe!'

stopping
can be scary

When she was well into her nineties, I asked my aunt what the secret of her long life was. Her reply? 'Masterful inactivity!' One of the most ancient ritualized ways of stopping is the Sabbath day in the Judaeo-Christian religion. The word Sabbath comes from the Hebrew for stopping or sitting. In the original biblical sources, it is defined as a day of stopping or resting. This is not inactivity, but halting the compulsive need to transform, fix, or improve things. It is a ritual reminder that the world is perfect, expressed in biblical language as the completion and perfection of creation on the seventh day. Ultimately, there is nothing that needs to be

done and we can honour the innate perfection of the world by taking one day for resting, appreciation and sacred stopping.

how do we calm
the body-mind?

When we think of slowing down, calming and relaxing, we usually assume that it relates to the body. So, let's start there. How do we calm the body? Obviously, we can relax deeply now and then, listen to music, breathe and tell the body to let go and be still. This will certainly calm the body and create a blessed pause in our stream of activity. But then we soon have to get up and go on. So, we need help to go deeper, to engage with the sources of restlessness and not just their expression, which will help us to embody calmness in our whole life. This is not about flopping into an armchair at every opportunity, nor shutting down our activity, exercise, energy and vital power. But it is about doing everything in life from a Calm centre. Imagine the simplest action, like reaching for our cup of tea. We can reach out and grab it with the automatic energy of grasping, driven by the dominant thought that we want the tea. Or we can make the same movement of the hand, which arises from our centre and continues with a soft internal intention until it joins the cup. It will be an utterly different experience. There will be a sense that we are in charge and we are calmly and consciously sending out the arm. Calmness is aligning ourselves with the source of action, not its result.

We experience agitation when we are pushed and pulled by impulses and needs and controlled by events to which we respond blindly, automatically and hastily. Our daily life activity can instead be filled with awareness and ease, driven by a steady internal engine, creating serenity. These are movements that are basic to Tai chi, Qigong and Aikido, but they can be as simple as the way we walk to the car.

Calmness is aligning ourselves with the source of action, not its result

One of the best ways to learn this is meditative walking or running or swimming. In walking, we can slow right down, so that each step is fully known and experienced from beginning to end. This is a classic practice used in Buddhist monasteries throughout the world. The monks walk up and down for hours, sometimes wearing a trench into the forest floor. This practice teaches the body and mind to shift into low gear or neutral, wake up out of automatic reactivity and to expand the consciousness right down to the feet. We don't need to walk at snail's pace to get the same results, nor do we need to be monks. If we are fully present while walking at a normal pace, or running, something happens to our whole body. The power of Mindfulness works. The body becomes filled with awareness – we know the feet moving, the legs, the breath, the movement of the whole body and the world moving alongside us. We are back in connection. There is nothing to chase and no place to get to. We will of course reach our goal, but in a different way, without the goal dominating our mind and body, creating pressure and haste.

In the famous Greek fables of the tortoise and the hare, the tortoise always gets there in the end, sometimes before the hare, but does so by being wise, slow and steady, without rushing. Of course, we sometimes need to move fast: we cannot be a tortoise when getting out of the way of a bus. But even when moving fast, if we are present the experience will have a different quality: swift, yet unimpeded and centred. How are we when we move? What is our body language? Do we move like a swan? A sparrow? A stork? An eagle? The Buddha was walking in the street one day and the dignity of his movement was so impressive that someone who met him stopped in amazement and said: 'Who are you? Are you a prince? Are you an angel? Are you a god?' 'No, said the

Buddha, I am not a prince, nor an angel, nor a god. I am simply awake!' The message is that this is not a learned dignity, like the training of aristocratic girls to walk slowly balancing a book on their head. It is an inner Calm and serenity that radiates outwards as an impressive presence and comes from mindful awareness and being awake to our movements. We will act with less grasping and the actions will feel more like they are doing themselves. Doing becomes non-doing.

One of the issues that make it difficult to slow down and do less, is that parts of us can slow down but other bits keep going like mad. The swan glides through the water most serenely, but have you ever seen what its webbed feet are doing beneath? They are paddling like crazy. Let's not be fooled by calmness on the surface and frantic paddling underneath. The human system is not one thing. Think of a situation of fear or anxiety: the body may be unmoving, but hormones are racing, muscles are tense and the mind is going at top speed, full of scripts and strategies.

I once saw a magazine cartoon of a woman sitting still in meditation. As she was sitting, there was a non-stop thought attack: 'what I still have to do', 'I shouldn't have said that', 'I am very worried about my daughter', 'how much is left in the bank', 'what happened yesterday was terrible', and on and on. At the end of an utterly exhausting forty-five minutes the teacher comes to her and says: 'Wasn't that relaxing, my dear?'

Calming the body will cascade throughout the whole being, but this is like the tail wagging the dog. The source of agitation and much of the ceaseless activity is built into the brain cells. It is the mind that needs to really relax and tell the body how to slow down, cool down, and calm down.

the still point

What stops our mind in its tracks, shuts us up and touches our heart with awe or sublime beauty? Is it the bright full moon emerging from behind the hills, a breath-taking multi-layered crimson sunset, or a majestic tree in the park or the sudden loving and deep look in the eyes of someone close to us? It can be a dramatic external experience that overwhelms the senses and stills the mind. Or it can be an internal spasm of insight that evolves into a deep and meaningful silence. Or the stillness after the storm, the space that opens up when crisis, laughter, or anger has dissipated. Or simply gaps in the stream of consciousness after sneezing, shouting, sleeping or orgasm. These situations show us that the chains of thoughts and chattering inner voices can be stilled naturally. How do we do this intentionally?

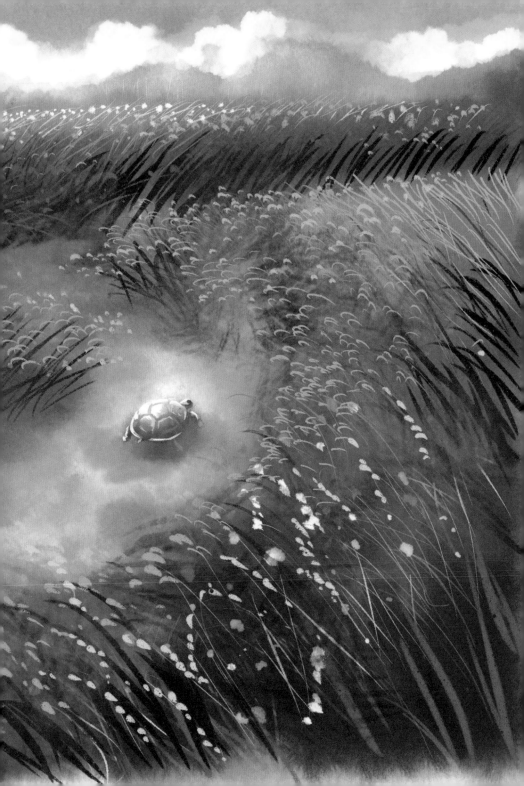

Perhaps the easiest way is by calming and quietening sensory content. Millions of people listen to recordings of quiet tones, meditative music and particularly, guided meditations. Another widespread option is guided deep relaxation, in which the soft tones of a yoga teacher, a recording, or our own inner voice, telling our body to relax and sink and soften, bit by bit, part by part, can be a very useful daily practice. It does quieten the whole system. But after a while we may get bored with the musical content, and we may just want the droning saccharin voice to shut up, or if the voice is attractive, we can find ourselves dependent on it to cool down and we can't slow down and centre ourselves without it. This is the time when we can let go of external means to slow us down and do it ourselves.

Meditation is the model for stopping. We can sit on the floor or on a chair or even an armchair, and let go of the urge to run, to do, or to jump up and look at our telephone. We can imagine that we sit as steadily as an unmovable rock in the stream and bring our attention to what it is that we are actually experiencing right now. This grounds us in awareness, in our sense of aliveness, of being and presence. We arrive back home where we actually live and find it is a place to rest and to be at ease. Once at home we continue by focusing on an aspect of our experience rather than the whole panoply. To use a traditional image, we watch the lotus, not the whole pond in which it grows.

starting points

Traditions from all over the world have ways of using an object to focus and calm the mind. In many Buddhist traditions it will be the image of a wheel, a coloured disk or a mandala. In some Indian traditions it will be a shiny stone with a point of light reflected on its surface. In yoga practice it is often simply a candle. Images can often be a helpful aid to concentration and Calm.

Very often the image might be internal, such as a point of light appearing in the mind, above and between the eyes in the location of 'the third eye'. Or it might be the image of a small star way up above the head. One very common starting point is subtle inner sounds. Called 'Nada' in the Indian tradition, they are background sounds that are usually ignored as we search for more meaningful sounds in the environment. They may be a relatively high-pitched inner tone or just a subtle vibration. In Sufi practice, chanting one strong syllable in time with the breath creates, with a bit of help from hyperventilation, a powerful focus.

Guided imagery is an inner journey to calmer, cooler and more expansive regions of the mind and heart. The use of images allows entrances into our inner world. They are the internal versions of chill-out music that can replace all the disturbing cacophony. Many images can help us settle ourselves. I once found myself in

front of a large group of students who were very keen to learn meditation but at first found it difficult to understand what to do. So I asked them to share with me their images of deep silence. They were delighted and enthusiastically described cultural images of the silence of the desert, the quietness of sitting under a date palm, of square-walled dwellings with a lemon tree as the still, quiet centre. Images regularly used to quieten the mind might be the steadiness of a rock in a stream of rushing water, or an ancient tree, rooted deeply in the earth, or a still pool of water that reflects the sky or indeed the image of our awareness as the sky, endless, spacious and free.

If we get up in the morning with a clear voice
that says *enough*, we should act on it.
We may need to go away, to shut up shop,
for the habits of constant doing may be so
strong that we need a radical change in our
circumstances to make a dent in them.

Calming the senses and deep concentration can settle our whole being into stillness. But for many of us this requires too much commitment and time. A more significant problem is that it shuts us down for a while, but then it finishes and the phone rings or we have to rush off to work. We may then find that, though the silence does have a beneficial influence on our day, it feels like a long-gone dream. We need to amplify and extend the Calm (Samadhi) with Mindfulness (Sati), so they both work in tandem and empower each other. As Mindfulness can be used throughout

the day or in any circumstances, we can invite Calm to ride piggy-
back into every corner of our life.

Mindfulness itself is a way to settle and steady our mind instead
of being scattered all over the place, driven by impulses, needs,
desires and habits. Slowly, we will begin to feel more connected
to ourselves and this reduces the need to escape from our hidden
dissatisfaction by ceaseless over-activity. We keep meeting our
centre, again and again and as we do this, we begin to feel we are
living from and in this centre rather than constantly outside of

ourselves, pushed and pulled by external conditions. This is how Calm is invited in along with Mindfulness.

It is actually our own nature that we are joining, just as if we go out to the forest or walk by the sea. The forest silences us because it takes us out of our heated selves. We become connected to a bigger space, where all is in its place and there is nothing to control or to change. Nature brings us a strong message of primal OK-ness and if we listen to this message, we will remember how to be content with what is. The trees remind us deeply what it is like to be silent, connected and happy with the way that we are. They teach us not to move about so much.

soothed by the breath

A very suitable location for our attention, helping to calm the system, is the breath, especially as experienced in the rising and falling of the belly, our centre of gravity. The advantage of using the breath and body as the address for concentration is that they are part of our life, they are natural and not artificial and they quite quickly and easily invite us into the now. We can't breathe in the past and the future.

We track and fully experience the expansion of the belly from the beginning of the in-breath, all the way, knowing the place where it turns and the whole journey to the contraction of the belly on the outbreath. We dive into the experience of breathing as if we are diving into deep waters or falling into a tunnel like Alice in Wonderland. We explore elements of the breath, its micro-texture, its modulations, the way each breath has its own original unique nature, without any history, like a line drawn on water. Focusing on the breath, we can get closer, more intimate with its subtle changing texture and it slows down. We penetrate the experience at the highest resolution we can, breaking down one breath into a journey; as it flows in from the outside, right through the body to the belly, energizing and filling our cells with life and then flows out again, with all the sensations, changes, small movements and feelings on the way. We softly ride the gentle flow of the breath in the body and as we do so, we find ourselves naturally slowing down, calming down and becoming centred and present. This is the way the two powers of Samadhi and Sati, Calm and Mindfulness, work together to nourish our inner Energy and bring us into a state of Trust.

We can extend the calming and focusing power of attention deeper and deeper, for ever extended periods. The gentle waves of in-breath and out-breath or the sensations flowing in the body then become a single object that draws us in. The closer we get to any

object, the more we zoom in, and the longer we stay there, the more everything slows down and becomes still. We find ourselves inside the ocean rather than being tossed by the waves on the surface.

keep your eye on the ball

For many of us, focus on a single unmoving object requires a great deal of effort and we can't keep it up for long. However, a similar result can be achieved by closely attending and tracking a moving object, not a static one. It is like watching a football match. The main instruction is to keep your eye on the ball! Try it out next time you watch a game. If we keep our eyes and attention on the movement of the ball, with awareness, we will find ourselves naturally developing that sharpness, focus, steadiness and power of samadhi. To some extent we already do this with focus on the breath or flow of sensation and touch experiences of the body, since they are constantly changing and shapeshifting. Try watching the clouds floating by; see what happens if you stay with them.

The question then arises: isn't this what I do anyway when I watch a good film or a football match, enthralled and hardly moving from my chair for a couple of hours? Isn't that experience the same as meditative concentration? The answer is no, and we should know the difference: when we watch a film or a football match we are sucked into and identify with the story or the action on the pitch. The attention is there but we are not. The story or the match has taken over or in our minds and there is no room left for mindful awareness. It is no difference from being lost in a story in our minds. But if we stay aware and present and at the same time follow one thing, such as the ball in the game, just as the breath, we are being both mindful and focused.

meeting the 'monkey mind'

Mindful awareness as part of our daily life and practice will gradually help us to live everyday with more serenity and steadiness. But it can take time. We can accelerate the process by directly meeting the source of all the ceaseless activity: the mind itself, jumping from thought to thought like a wild monkey leaping from branch to branch. It is the monkey mind, chattering and babbling, cheering and jeering that keeps grabbing our attention and running off with it.

The monkey creates pandemonium because that way he keeps us entranced by his theatrical show. Instead of us capturing and taming the monkey, the monkey has captured us. One way to reverse this and central to Mindfulness practice, is to keep stepping out of the theatre. We step back from the play, reduce identification with the story and step into a more total sensory receptivity. We know our body, the space in the theatre, the lights and the sounds. We may be captivated by the stream of consciousness, but it is always possible to take a couple of breaths and invite in the sound of the birds outside the window. Through direct sensory awareness we return to our quiet centre. This skill in frequently and easily stepping out of the show, even if the monkeys grab us and pull us back in a hundred times, gradually quietens the monkeys as they accept that they are losing their audience. It is not that easy to exit the theatre. So it can be helpful at times to stay there, allow the drama to play out in our minds, but keep it as background, where it doesn't capture us so much. Our stories become ripples of thoughts that chat to themselves out there somewhere, small clouds passing across the sky, like the sound of traffic in the street, or the sound of children playing in the nearby playground. This establishes a new relationship with the mind, in which we are less the puppet controlled by its every whim. An issue or narrative that arises turns into background music, instead of being, as Shakespeare has Macbeth so memorably described it: '... a tale. Told by an idiot, full of sound and fury, signifying nothing'.

Replace *to-do* with *to-be*

At other times we do need to engage more closely with the play so that we can rewrite the script. We can zoom in on the engines that drive this ceaseless activity, such as the to-do lists in the mind. We will see the habits of restlessness and agitation, experience the discomfort that they bring, but just stay with it. The sense of pressure and disturbance of the rushing river of the mind and the longing for peace and stillness, is our teacher. It shows us deeply the unsatisfying nature of all this mental drama. Mental habits are fully seen and we can actively let them go, as if to say to them: 'OK. I've seen you. I've got the point. Thank you and goodbye'. When such content exits stage left, a small space opens up, which is very important: it is a mental window into simple awareness instead of commenting and conceiving. We find ourselves sitting quietly in our place and doing nothing. And it's no problem. It feels just fine. The monkeys' antics, when watched with curiosity and detachment, are revealed as pointless and habitual. By coming out from under the control of the busy mind, we take away the fuel from its engine and feed our quiet steadiness instead. We begin to reframe our to-do list as a to-be list.

Can you imagine how it would feel to live with unshakeable peace and serenity? How would you get up in the morning and how would you act at work, and with what eyes would you look at those closest to you? What is needed in your life for this to happen? It would be natural to think that peace would come if you were less disturbed by external events. But that is not real peace, since external circumstances are beyond our control and the world is a difficult place. Experiences of stillness would also not be enough, however beautiful and beneficial they may be, because they too come and go. We would need a deep and harmonious connection with ourselves to discover palpable peace. If you consider moments of quiet contemplation and realization in your own life, you will notice that they always go along with peacefulness. The wise sage is not agitated. Insight, getting close to life, beckons peace.

In this way, stillness can lead directly to the fifth power – that of Wisdom – and peace, if it is combined with a deep listening to the voices that were buried under layers of habitual thinking. We need to engage with them. Contemplation and concentration can open channels and expose what is hidden. As Rumi wrote:

Why are we so afraid of silence?
Silence is the root of everything.
If you spiral into its void
A hundred voices will thunder
Messages you long to hear.

Stillness allows us to see deeply. The power of a steady mind focuses the eye of Mindfulness, which can then reveal other levels, as the stillness of a pool of water without ripples allows us to see to the bottom. There may be mud down there, the accumulated silt and sediment of our life, which create our everyday thoughts, responses, struggles and insights. But maybe we can also see jewels glittering, multicoloured fish swimming. We are no longer just experiencing what is on the surface but are constantly receiving the gifts from the depths and they make us rich. We will also come to appreciate the power of the steady mind itself, not just what it reveals. Water that hides diamonds sparkles like them.

Once we have established the breath as a place of quiet focus, we may move to sensations and feelings in the body. We note places of contraction, tension or discomfort and places of ease and comfort. The calmness is like arriving home. We go into long-unvisited rooms and stop to take in their novel and engrossing contents. We will be helped by an attitude of curiosity and interest, like a scientist fascinated by what becomes visible under the microscope. Kindness too should be our partner: soft caring attention may reveal a contraction in the chest area as an unconscious fear or anger that was deeply buried. As it emerges as a feeling, memory or story, it is released and peace takes its place.

calm and insight:
twins at play

The power of Calm and the power of Wisdom are, in the traditional images, like two wings of a bird flying towards liberation, or like two sheaves of wheat leaning on each other. Calm works from the outside in, Wisdom from the inside out and the two meet in peace and harmony. We may find ourselves irritated, disturbed,

frustrated or disappointed without understanding why. The reason will lie in the invisible world of unconscious tendencies and psychological patterns, the deep insecurities and wounds that we do not fully know and we do not readily see the ways and means to dissolve. However, we can see them when they arise to the surface as mind-body signs, for example as agitation and restlessness. We calmly focus and concentrate our inner awareness, like a laser, at these signs. They give way under our gaze, and with this power of focused attention they reveal what is going on underneath. Our

patterns are exposed, our tendencies softened and befriended and we can let them be and let them go.

On one retreat a psychoanalyst came to me for a one-on-one meeting. A round-faced middle-aged man, with heavy glasses and a calm, jovial, manner, he was very chatty at first, smiled a lot, saying how much he appreciated the retreat and the practice. Given his profession, these positive statements seemed to be an ego strategy to help him feel better about coming to me with a problem. I waited, ready for the sting that was obviously in the tail of all these compliments. Eventually, after some prodding, he said, with evident discomfort, that he was getting bored with his clients. He felt restless listening to them. He would look at his watch, thinking of what he wanted to do the next day. He felt a deep urge to escape and sometimes that grew into a palpable anxiety or even a sense of panic, especially because he felt guilty about these feelings.

I suggested that he use the infallible duet of Calm and insight. He could find a bodily phenomenon that was easy for him, particularly the breath in the stomach, dropping into its soft rhythm, letting panic, restlessness and resistance all settle down. When he felt calmer, he could allow the awareness to spread from his own body to that of the other person, including both of them in a Calm presence. He would feel himself more engaged, more able to listen deeply and less needing to escape. Awareness would create intimacy. Intimacy would open his heart and compassion and concern might arise naturally for himself as well as for the client. He would feel quieter, settled and open. At the same time, whenever the feelings of restlessness and resistance did occur, he could mindfully turn to them as a friend, not an enemy and listen deeply to their voices, wherever they could be heard: in the body, in the feeling tones, in the mind's stories. Knowing them to be a natural expression of some inner pain, he could let them arise, reveal themselves and let them pass.

Impatience and frustration are very human qualities. They are primary sources of pressure and stress and completely steal our peace. When we are late for a meeting and stuck in a traffic jam, who would be cool, relaxed and at ease? If there are issues in our life that we are desperate to resolve, who wouldn't be frustrated on occasion? Impatience is based on a dissatisfaction that we are not always aware of, keeping us relentlessly chasing what we want to achieve or what we think ought to happen. One of the best examples of this is competitiveness. On the one hand, competition is seen as essential to evolution, essential to success and growth and a backbone of western civilization and economy. Even competition with ourselves – how we want ourselves to be vis a vis how we are – is seen as a healthy form of growth and development.

Though it can on occasion be helpful in energizing our life, competitiveness blocks peace and is not actually needed for growth, development, success and happiness. We can use up our whole life and energy in the service of competition and arrive at the end of our life questioning whether it was all worth it. There are better ways, such as the joy and creativity of manifesting our gifts. Even evolution can be looked at in this way – rather than the survival of the fittest, it is the fruits of life's creative Energy.

We may feel frustrated and alarmed when we look around and see so much inequality, injustice, ecological catastrophe and plain heartlessness. We feel the urgent need to go out and make change. We should listen to our heart and sometimes we can be energized by righteous anger. But in the long run, this may not be so helpful to others or ourselves and we may be more effective by being steadier and more patient.

how to wait

Patience needs to be melted to fill our body, mind and heart with the beautiful quality of quiet and composure, from which we act at the appropriate time and pace. Who would you want to rescue

you in an emergency or operate on you in surgery: someone who stays Calm and equanimous, or someone impatient and irritated?

In the world of spiritual practice, it is a common concept to wait for grace from God. The desert fathers of early Christianity called it Expectatas. The Sufi metaphor for this is patiently sitting at the doorstep of the Sheikh, waiting for the door to open. There is something beautiful but at the same time painful in longing and hoping for revelation from elsewhere or an external source. If your state of grace must come from 'above', as an act of God, then all you can do is wait for it. But if grace comes from within the heart of your experience, as in Buddhist awareness practice, then you don't need to wait for anything or expect anything. Every bit of awareness peels back layers of conditioning and reveals innate freedom and grace in this moment, happening constantly. It is true that much is beyond our control, but this is a source of Wisdom rather than expectation. There is nothing to wait for. It is all here if we notice it.

In its deeper sense, patience is an invitation to stillness; more about being than waiting. We rest in the experience of the moment rather than being driven by what we want to happen in the future, or by habits we built in the past. As we sit in the traffic jam, understanding that uncontrollable life created all the conditions that made this moment as it is. We can just sit back, relax, let go of any pressure, drop into the life of body, mind and world, welcoming things just as they are.

We may assume that we can win calmness by keeping life at bay; that we can keep our inner core undisturbed like a non-stick pan from which everything rolls off. This is like trying to still the pool of water by making sure that no stones are thrown into it. Unfortunately, this is not a solution, as keeping life at a distance and avoiding disturbance is itself a disturbance; we have to work at it and maintain psychological shields and defences. We will be quite occupied mentally, emotionally, and physically with avoiding difficult experiences and we will be investing in denial. For example, in relationships with partners, denial or avoidance of difficulty creates a superficial calm, but it can produce suppressed anger and distance and is a major source of breakups. Whereas consciously confronting difficulties together, being in the same boat while riding the stormy waves, invites intimacy and so is one of the major sources for healing and togetherness.

An age-old criticism of the spiritual life is that it is all very well for meditators, monks and yogis to explore deep peace, calmness and personal liberation, but they do so by shutting out the real world, which is a noisy mess and just indulge themselves in a narcissistic and secluded self-development. There can be some truth in this. Spiritual communities can get self-centred, exclusive and cut off. We ourselves can easily fall into the illusion that spiritual development is inner work and we need to win peace by shutting the door and not engaging with others or confronting life's challenging aspects.

There may indeed be situations where protection and even denial is a wise choice, particularly if the pain is overwhelming and we do not have the means to handle it. I once gave a course to a group who were all above seventy years of age. One elderly gentleman told me that he had been through the Holocaust as a child. He said he loved the inner peace of the practice and was ready to meet and work with any and all the pains of life. But not that one. That one, he said, was out of this room. That was wise. But it may not be easy to decide when it is wise and appropriate to choose Calm and quiet even at the cost of denial or switching off and when we need to meet our demons head on. What about when we feel besieged by bad news or just overstimulated by information and can't look at any more media? Or when we are going through a sensitive period and we just need to stay at home and not face a crowded city centre? Or when we feel we do not have the strength to see a certain person or family member, knowing it will be a difficult and challenging meeting?

A useful rule of thumb in such situations would be to examine the level and capacity of each of The Five Powers within us, the power to be mindful, to be steady, to be heartful and trusting, to be energetic and to be wise and reflective. If we decide we have enough of these tools to work with the situation, we can go for it. However, if we feel the situation to be totally overwhelming, we can allow wise withdrawal and defence, in the name of calmness.

In the end, however, we cannot find real peace by shutting out the world. It doesn't work. Peace will escape us if it is conditional. The world will creep back in through the back door and disturb us from there. Serenity and equanimity are very beautiful and refined states of mind and heart, but they are definitely not indifference. They let the world in. Indifference keeps the world out.

We need to surf the waves of life, calmly, safely and easily, rather than insulating ourselves from them in an air-conditioned nearby resort. The key is a life of equanimity. But how can we be equanimous if we are constantly invaded by difficulties, struggle, pain and disappointment and allow the suffering of ourselves and others to penetrate to our core without putting up our habitual defences? It may seem an impossible mission.

We cannot find real peace by shutting out
the world

equanimity:
steady like the earth

As we go deeper into the power of Calm, we begin to realize that all the disturbances of life are in our mind, not in itself. Our mind has decided that one sound – an ambulance passing by – is an invasion, while another – a babbling brook – is a delight. It is our mind that perceives cacophony; it's not in the poor decibels, which are just sound waves doing their thing. We are disturbed because we are disturbable.

It is the same with everything that arrives at the doorways of our senses. It is our perception and interpretation that then create reactivity or receptivity, anger or love, acceptance or rejection, comfort or discomfort. And our interpretation is heavily coloured by our needs, interests and concerns, all grounded in our struggle to survive. Equanimity is a deep steadiness in which we are unshakeable, not because of well-developed defences, nor because of indifference. Our mind is open, light and free: we are less wrapped up in ourselves and our compulsion to survive. We allow pleasant and unpleasant experiences to come and go, but they do not work inside us, creating waves and eliciting habitual reactivity. They just pass through, like light through a glass. We can be vulnerable and sensitive, yet never knocked down; ready to welcome whatever comes our way. Equanimity is a powerful state that can emanate to others and calm them when in crisis, whether through a few words or just by silently modelling a different state. Once during a workshop I was leading on conflict all hell broke loose and everyone started shouting at each other. I felt that I had lost it, so I sat silently in the middle and waited for it to settle down, which it did after a few minutes. I was surprised when the co-facilitator thanked me for my calming Energy. Only in retrospect did I understand that I had been broadcasting equanimity and it had worked.

How do we develop such unshakeable equanimity? Actually, all The Five Powers – indeed, the entire body of Buddhist spiritual practice – lead here; it is the fruit of every little bit of mindful awareness and the expansive, trusting heart. As we turn towards and receive experience without preference or manipulation, whether pleasant or unpleasant, we purify the mind of its habits of needing to control things and we become bigger than and undisturbed by all the dynamic dualities of life.

There are also specific practices that help develop equanimity. One traditional method is to use phrases that are said repeatedly, especially when faced with challenging circumstances and they rewrite the usual mental scripts based on insecurity. These might include: 'May I accept things as they are' or: 'May I be undisturbed by the coming and going of events'.

It needs to be emphasized that as long as we hold on to an assumed sense of me in here and an uncontrollable world out there, it is inevitable that there will some level of noise and disturbance. Equanimity is the peak of our spiritual journey, because it is the way we might live if we deconstruct or dissolve this sense of me and mine, selfhood, ego and subject. If we hold ourselves more lightly, we will be able to dance with uncontrollable life rather than struggle against it. There will be no one there to be disturbed.

A man came to the bank of a river and asked a boatman to take him across. In mid-stream their vessel was hit by another. The boatman shouted at the man guiding the other craft, berating him as an idiot who should take care where he was going. As they continued on their journey, they were struck by an empty boat. The boatman remained silent. The passenger asked him why he did not shout like last time, and the boatman replied that there was no one to shout at. Can we be like that empty boat, floating downstream, no one to be shouted at?

Being empty is not all or nothing: bit-by-bit, as we grow and develop spiritually, we find greater lightness, transparency and spaciousness. And the spaciousness is both within and without. We live with a sense of intimacy with and immersion into the world. As this occurs, equanimity grows naturally and deeply, for we cannot be disturbed by the world if we are the world. Who can disturb whom? With that level of inner spaciousness, we will

be able to take more and more pain and suffering for ourselves or others. This is the secret of spiritual teachers who are able to listen deeply to endless suffering of living beings but because of inner emptiness cannot be drowned or overwhelmed by it. It is symbolized by the Buddha's long ears in Buddhist iconography.

peace in the
eye of storm

Stillness is like the eye of the storm. We reach it through the storm of life, which always has a calm centre. What is it like in the eye of the storm? What is it like to abide there? It is not a deadness or a switching off. It is a place of quiet potential where life arises and we ourselves are the calm centre. We experience stillness in a turning world.

But we can go further. If disturbance is in our response to the world and not in the world itself, then the storm too is a perception and not a reality. There is much more stillness in life than we realise. A word or a thought is only known because it comes out of silence and returns to it. Sound is heard because it is different from the silence that preceded it, otherwise we could not hear it. We only notice movement because movement is of one thing relative to another and that is all our mind is trained to see. We don't notice the silence and the stillness because we give sound and movement all the attention, just as we don't notice the space in a room because we are only interested the objects, or we don't see light itself, only what is lit.

But if we cleanse our 'doors of perception', as William Blake describes them, our awareness would become more inclusive and 'everything would appear to man as it is, Infinite'. We could pay attention to the silence within and around things, as much as the things themselves. Can we notice the white paper on which these words are written? It is blank, silent and undisturbed by the words that it permits, just as the screen is undisturbed by the images projected onto it, the sky is undisturbed by the clouds floating by. The ocean creates the waves but is undisturbed by them, and our expanded awareness is the source of, and is undisturbed by, the thoughts that arise from it.

At the heart of our experience of thoughts, concepts and objects of the world there is the knowing itself, which is constantly reaching out and seeking the objects that are to be known. This knowing, this ground of awareness, is still and endless like space or the ocean. As much as we can come home and rest in that primal awareness, like a bird coming home to roost, we will find there unlimited peace.

The Fifth Power

Wisdom

Pannya

WISDOM | INSIGHT | AWAKENING

Our lives are flooded. From morning to night, we are besieged by information. We have very little chance to weigh up what really matters, what makes a difference to our life.

Our drive for more knowledge is a double-edged sword: the kind of knowledge required to grow a beloved flower garden, to play fine music, to write or read poetry, to appreciate and know what is happening on this earth and under this sky, is beautiful and precious. We also need to know the best treatment for a health problem and the times of the train we want to catch. But much knowledge is tied in to concerns, anxieties, needs and protection. We are endlessly driven to work out how to improve or secure our lives and cope with the challenges that come streaming in every day. This knowledge can trap us in a limited world, based on a need to control what arises from uncertainty. No one wants to go back to the time before antibiotics, yet this intractable drive to be in control is also hugely destructive and is now destroying nature and the life it was meant to preserve.

how to
recognize wisdom

What kind of understanding would we need to live more lightly, to take responsibility for our life and our minds and direct ourselves to wholesome, beneficial and liberated horizons? It would certainly be more immediate, more intuitive, more insightful and more spacious than regular thinking. It is a state of constant awareness. It is a deep understanding of the immensity of our being. It is the extraordinary in the heart of the ordinary. It tends to be non-conceptual, non-verbal and has a quality of immediate clarity. It reads and senses the inter-relationships between us and the world. It is a deep listening to what our inner voices are telling us and a sensing of what is happening at this moment. It is humble and quiet. It asks a question and lets go of expectations for an answer, but trusts the question to work in the background and bring what is needed in its wake. It reads the tweets sent by life. The great poet Wordsworth offers a beautiful description of Wisdom:

While with an eye made quiet by the power
Of harmony, and the deep power of joy,
We see into the life of things.

going beyond
regular thinking

Wisdom is not the same as intense thinking, though it is easy to get the two confused. We tend to turn things round and round in our minds trying to work out what will make us happier and more contented. Yet there is something deeply unsatisfying about rumination. It can drive us farther, not closer, from truth and understanding, uses a lot of energy and may disconnect us from the world. It is a rather uncomfortable truth that all the thinking, strategizing and planning about how to be happier doesn't do the job.

Wisdom begins where regular thinking gets stuck. It is a kind of knowing that frees us, that brings more ease, happiness and insight into our life. It is helpful to us and those around us. Wisdom always reduces, rather than increases suffering. All of us are attracted to the wise – they emanate something that settles us and gives us hope and they are constantly cheerful and steady, even in difficult circumstances. Think of a wise figure in your own life and how they can heal and inspire others by the reflective and big-hearted Energy they emanate. Wisdom welcomes us into a richer, broader, oceanic place where we can find a deep fulfilment.

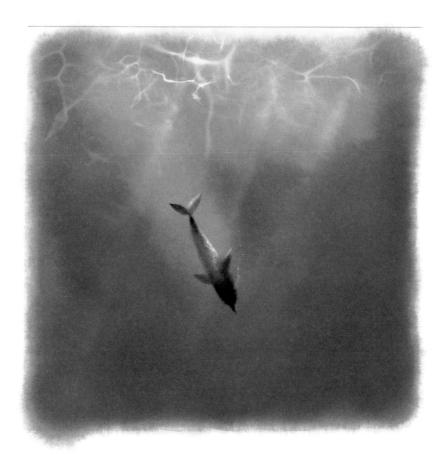

Of course, thinking has incredibly power - the mind that can conceive the nature of galaxies light years away can be wise as well as clever. But it is not necessarily so. Generally, if we explore life with intensity, if we are in love with the unknown, we will find ourselves leaping beyond thinking and cleverness into Wisdom. There is a Tibetan proverb: 'if you are too clever, you can miss the point entirely'.

Every one of us has seeds of Wisdom: the quiet inner voice that calls us to look again, the longing to understand what is really going on, the search for our truth and the occasional greatness of spirit and kind-heartedness that surprise even ourselves. These seeds need to be watered and fed by our respect, attention and appreciation. They need to be given space to grow.

We can develop Wisdom by working with the other powers: Trust, Mindfulness, Energy and Calm, all of which bear fruit in Wisdom, the fifth power. Each power, when explored, will take us on a journey beneath and beyond the habitual tracks of the mind. For example, Mindfulness or any meditative practice will tend to bring more space, awareness and clarity to the mind and ready it for insights to emerge. With calmness and collectedness (Samadhi) we will be able to look at what arises with a steady gaze: in the words of Wordsworth, 'see into the life of things'. We will find ourselves diving below the surface into an unimagined ocean teeming with strange and wonderful beings.

reigniting our enquiring mind

We need to know where to look, how to let go and dive in and what experiences to watch for on the way. However, we are faced with a fundamental obstacle. From childhood, we are fed with opinions, views and knowledge by parents, teachers and elders. Even our inner world tends to be shaped by others. We need a genuine longing for something beyond the second-hand truths that we were fed, a hunger to search, to enquire, to look beneath the surface of things, to be ready to touch the unknown and the invisible and not the pre-digested facts and knowledge that is all around us. There is something radical in this search, since it does not stop with conventional truths, consensus views, authority, dogmas or traditional texts.

There is a traditional Buddhist text, the Kalama Sutta, that is often called 'The Charter of Free Inquiry'. A group called the Kalamas told the Buddha that they were being given so many conflicting views and teachings that they no longer knew what they should do or believe. The Buddha answered that they should not go according to what everybody says, nor according to tradition, nor according to assumptions, rumour or beliefs, nor upon the holy books, nor according to faith in a teacher. Rather, when they themselves found that a certain way led to benefit and happiness for them and others and was praised by the wise, they should pursue it unstintingly. Instead of endlessly studying sacred texts, says the Zen poet Ikkyu, 'we should learn how to read the love letters sent by the wind, and rain, the snow and moon'.

where is
our wisdom?

In the search for realization and a helpful path, as advised by the Kalama Sutta, we may find ourselves looking in far away and in exotic places. We travel long distances, cross the seas and fly round the world in search of it. We long for it in the future or cry for a lost Wisdom in the past and of course look for it at the feet of a great teacher. The search for the sources of Wisdom somewhere else can sometimes be exactly what is needed to kick-start a spiritual journey. External inspiration can trickle in and lead to internal transformation.

I have benefitted hugely in my own journey from teachers whose words hit home, starting with Alan Watts and Krishnamurti half a century ago. However, in the end the truth we seek at the temple is the truth that we brought there in the first place but had

forgotten that we had it. The Biblical Book of Job asks: 'Where can Wisdom be found?... not in me, said the abyss, not in me said the oceans...'. Job eventually awakens to the source of Wisdom, which is in a deep seeing of nature. The teacher, if they know their business, will be a mirror to show us our own Wisdom that was overlooked. There is no need to run elsewhere to see more clearly. There is plenty of need to dive inside our soft open centre, abide there and listen to the quiet voices that we usually ignore. Wisdom is in the ordinary. It is ordinary magic that is revealed by consistent Mindfulness and presence, or indeed any of the

powers. Washing the dishes with awareness of our body and mind and the feelings that pass through us; with care and quietness in our actions, we directly invite Wisdom to unfold. The power of faith and Trust would show us that this moment and its activity is just what should be and cannot be something else or better; we let go and drop into this moment and its activity. Then the emerging Wisdom may be felt as the joy of being alive, the awareness of the preciousness of this moment; its originality, its fullness and the connectedness it brings between ourselves and the whole world.

In other words, the only place to find freedom and liberation is inside the experience of the moment. It is in the heart of our experience, but it is covered over by layers of habit and conditioning that need to be peeled off. The Tibetans use the image of a mud sculpture that conceals a gold sculpture hidden within. If we unpeel layers of automatic interpretations, assumptions and beliefs, we will find in the core of any experience unimagined awareness.

Let's take the most ordinary example of planning thoughts, which tend to take over our mind and circle round and round as imagined strategies. They can be about how to get somewhere, write something, make something, say something, succeed at something, or just what to cook for dinner tonight. Thought will be busy weaving possible tracks and checking each one according to the imagined goal. If we are living on automatic pilot, this process will be spinning round inside us and we will be entirely unconscious of it, a bit like constantly re-arranging the furniture. But if we scratch the surface and apply the powers, we will begin to bring all this mental activity into the light of day. We will see that we are trapped by habit-driven circles in the mind. We may notice that it is a bit annoying, contracted, limited, filling the mind with unnecessary content. Like junk.

Once we wake up to that, we can go further and realise that the whole chain of obsessive thinking is just chains of thought passing by, each with a beginning and an end and not at all an endless uninterrupted stream. We might realise that after all they are just thoughts; we can give them a label as the well-worn planning mind and let them pass by like clouds in the sky. We can also realise that we never actually gave those thoughts permission: they arrived by themselves in response to external conditions that demanded from us a response and elicited a need to do something.

We were never really in charge. We can step back, step out and shove both the thoughts and the thinker off centre stage. As a result, we will feel far less bound, we will invest less energy in cerebral circles, our mind will soften and lighten, our heart may be touched, we will discover an inner spaciousness and we can be more reflective. We can then do what needs to be done, in all probability more effectively, since most of the excessive thinking was like pressing the gas pedal in neutral.

the squirrel and the blackbird

One day I was standing in a park in London and watching an old man throwing nuts to a squirrel, one by one. The first nuts were eaten. But after that the squirrel took each nut, dug a little hole and buried it. Then he got another nut, went forward a few paces and buried that one. He continued running a few paces, burying a nut, running a few more paces, burying another nut and so on. The squirrel didn't realise that behind him was a large blackbird. Every time the squirrel buried a nut and moved on, the blackbird dug it up and ate it.

We are so painfully like the squirrel, carrying on blithely as if what we do, what we accumulate, we ourselves, will last for ever, ignoring the utter fragility, unpredictability and temporariness of everything. The blackbird, especially its blackness, reminds us of the Grim Reaper following us. This is a powerful image of ignorance, of ignoring the truth of things. We live automatically, filling our daily round with coping, expectations, plans, beliefs and so on, trying to beat this uncontrollable life that keeps pulling the rug out from under our feet. Frustration, anxiety and dissatisfaction are our desserts. Most of us do have our personal escape hatches in which we can leave behind or cover over these existential concerns, for a while. They may be in the shape of our smart phones, entertainment, distractions, relationships or intoxicants. Of course they are not always escapes, but if they are we will recognize them as such because they will not bring real relief, they tend to drain our powers such as Energy and vitality rather than replenish them and we will mostly feel that after the film is over and we have turned off the screen, we will be back where we started. In the end, only a deep and enduring Wisdom will allow us to abide in harmony, contentment and peace despite all that life throws at us.

lotus in the mud

The wise heart does not hide from, cover up or deny our vulnerability and fundamental lack of safety. It knows that we cannot rely or depend on anything, as all changes and passes on. It is ready to look our fundamental insecurity straight in the eyes. You might ask, how on earth can that make us a happier person, even if things don't work or the body gets sick? The surprising fact is that if we live with this truth it brings more joy, not more suffering. We understand that life can only be fully lived in the unfolding now, whatever it brings, as there is no other place to live. A classic image of this is the lotus, beautiful and pure, growing out of the muddy pool that is our life. Living on the edge brings us unimagined freedom and wellbeing. This is one of the reasons wise sages are always cheerful. There is a Zen story of the man who falls over a cliff and just manages to hang on to a clump of grass to save himself. His weight is gradually pulling the clump of grass out at the roots; he could fall to his death at any moment. Is that a strawberry growing out of the cliff face? Oh my! How delicious!

seeing with new eyes

Wisdom needs a beginner's mind. Like the boy in the fairy tale, who is prepared to shout out "the Emperor is naked"! We too can be ready to look at life directly, clearly and honestly. We no longer run with the herd, believing the consensus. Wisdom is to be wide awake in the midst of our life. Waking up means waking from sleep. Sleep does not necessarily mean anaesthesia, depression or boredom, although it can be any of these. It is sleepwalking through our life, as if under an enchantment,

acting out our life mechanically, constantly occupied with managing, coping and trying to be comfortable. Waking up will reveal everything as fresh, new and surprising. This is not about collecting new experiences. It is about seeing everything with new eyes. We are kicked out of the routine into a world of amazement, where everything matters. As T.S Eliot said:

'*We shall not cease from exploration*
And the end of all our exploring
Will be to arrive where we started
And know the place for the first time.'

The place to move from the sleep of automatic living to the wakefulness of the Wisdom mind is in the heart of our experience. The method is seeing under the surface with Mindfulness, Trust, a kind heart and authentic inquiry. What then are the insights that liberate? In the previous example of the planning mind, can we pick out what exactly was revealed when we peeled back the layers of conditioned responses? We can identify three basic insights that, according to the classic Buddhist teachings, are called the Three Seals, Three Marks, or Three Characteristics.

The first is dukkha (in Pali), dissatisfaction. When we look clearly at the experience of a contracted consciousness tied up in cycles of thought, we see that it is unpleasant and confining. If we look closely at any ordinary experience, such as a notion, thought, perception, view or response, we may be surprised to

find that there is a subtle edge of dissatisfaction about it, mostly because it will be constructed, fixed, and bounded.

For example, when we have an opinion, a close examination may reveal that there is mild discomfort in the belief in our own rightness, in others being wrong and in our need to hold the notion as an incontrovertible fact. This of course, becomes more obvious if the experience is of something unpleasant and painful such as a backache, a heartache, a disappointment, a loss, an irritation or a struggle. We can explore the nature of the pain, listen to its real voice, where and how and what it is like, what we do with it, and what stories we build around it. The truth of underlying dukkha can show us the needs, pressures, pains, and dissatisfactions that drive much of our life from below. It can be a teacher that shows us our limits, and if we engage at eye level with unpleasant experiences and become their interested friend rather than aversive enemy, we will find that we can be their master, not their slave. They will be less dominant and overwhelming and less intense. We will not feel the victim and we can enjoy a full life along with them.

A middle-aged lady in one of my classes suddenly burst into tears during a guided meditation. At the end of the class she said that for years she had had chronic hip pain and been taking medication and she was also serving a big family and a demanding husband. She said she felt a lifelong victim and servant. Suddenly, when she was looking directly at the hip pain, it simply vanished and she cried as she realised that she could do something to help herself. It made her feel empowered.

It's not just bad news that opens the doors of insight; the good news does too. We also engage with the joy, happiness, and pleasant experiences at eye level. In doing so, we realise how unpleasant and pleasant are both sources of dependence, stories, narratives and responses. We can let them go and gradually realise that we are bigger than both the pleasant and unpleasant, the 'oy' and the joy, that come and go relative to each other.

experience
is a line
drawn on water

The second Characteristic of all experience that opens the Wisdom mind is Anicca, transience. Nothing is fixed, all experience is a flow, a dynamic changing movement. To use the example of planning, mindful awareness would see the thoughts of strategies and scenarios chasing each other and zipping by like fast-moving clouds in the sky. Take the example of grasping a cup of tea. An unexamined experience would just direct the hand, make sure it grasped correctly, and that the triangle – me, cup and hand – were all coordinated. End of story. But close examination of the experience would show that the touch of the hand on the cup and the grasping is a whole universe of indescribable sensations of touch, pressure, warmth and movement that constantly changes, including varied experiences of different fingers. Hand, cup and the controlling self are just seen as summaries and instead there

is a changing field of undefinable living sensations that is never still for one moment. This is out of the box. A magical world opens, vast and flowing like a great river. Every experience is like a line drawn on water; a castle made of sand that melts back into the sea.

This brings us straight into the liberating sense of nowness, presence. It is all happening and unfolding in front of us right now and then vanishing. The step I take at this moment has a beginning and an end and in between is a whole journey. The thought I am having at this moment arises from nothing, goes back to nothing and in between signifies the world.

The third of the three Characteristics or Marks is Anatta, non-self. This is a paradoxical and confusing teaching. Yet it cannot be ignored, since it is a cornerstone of any authentic journey to a more liberated and insightful life. What is driving our life? What is it that we are defending when we are in conflict, that fuels our endless struggles and neediness, that is behind the need to control experience, that is occupied with success and failure, that sustains psychological patterns and narratives and gets stuck in habits? It is the assumption of the 'me' inside that not only seems to be running the show but is also the filter through which we are forced to see everything and which blocks the bigger Wisdom view.

The self, which is the total sense of identity, ego, ownership and boundary is like our operating system. We all need a healthy operating system, otherwise we will get knocked down by the first car when attempting to cross the road. On the other hand, when we are not mindful, the self dominates our life: we are constantly busy defending ourselves, occupied with satisfying its every need and whim, obeying its dictates and generally serving it when it should be serving us. It is meant to protect the body, but it ends up doing little other than protecting itself. And this can end up

with exactly the opposite result, with the body held hostage and sacrificed to the caprices of the self, for example, when violence breaks out because of an affront to honour and dignity.

A sweet story by the Russian author Kirillov illustrates the often-absurd domination of our self-story. A horse was stuck in the mud and managed, after a huge and heroic effort to pull itself free. As it freed itself, a fly flew from its tail and proudly proclaimed: 'we did it!'. The self is mostly invisible to us, we just do it or are it and see through it. We are like a king in his castle, made of thick walls, but believing that we rule a huge kingdom, not noticing that we are in fact imprisoned behind walls. If we can

begin to get a glimpse of how this self assumes control and runs our life, we can open windows in the walls and let in the light. We realise that the self is less solid and pre-existing than we thought. It is more of a verb than a noun, a fluid response to circumstances, not a thing, a process not an entity.

For this to happen we need to get glimpses of this self in action, which needs insight and clarity and Calm, the penetrating gaze on our life that is the province of The Five Powers. We can see how the sense of self balloons like an air bag when someone threatens, challenges or argues with us, and how it becomes an excruciating nagging voice when we need to make difficult decisions and how it transforms into a tyrant when we set our goals. At the same time we sense it soften when there is no need for it, when we sit by the sea or stroll in the woods or relax deeply. It gets out of the way when we are deeply concentrated in meditation or creativity. Wisdom grows when we begin to witness the self as a pervasive but dynamic and transparent presence.

It is important that we don't get stuck on any theory, dogma, or assumption about the self or non-self. We should let go of any concept that the self does or does not exist, which will get us marooned in a belief system. Whenever the Buddha was questioned directly if the self exists or not, he was silent. He explained that if he said it existed it would lead to the erroneous belief that the self, the 'me' is something, an entity or an object. If he said it did not exist, it would run counter to our experience and lead to beliefs in nihilism.

When we try and find the self as an entity, an object of awareness, we cannot. In Winnie the Pooh, Pooh was looking for Piglet somewhere and made the comment that the more he looked, the more he was aware of Piglet's absence. As a child, I remember looking at myself in the mirror for hours, and seeing hands, clothes, hair, teeth, nose and all the other bits. But I just couldn't see me myself there. It was a puzzle. The way to work with self is to watch it in operation, witnessing the multiple identities and the mystery of who we really are. We can view and know the sense of self and identity as a kaleidoscope of fascinating colours and shapes, constantly changing according to circumstances, sometimes vanishing. It is like a transparent partner that accompanies us wherever we go.

As we look carefully at our experiences, worlds open that we couldn't see when we looked at everything through the filter of me and mine. If we look at our body, for example, we can watch how much of life is just doing itself, wondrously, without our control. Again and again we can experience the profound and liberating awareness that life is happening by itself. All we need to do is to welcome and allow it. This is a huge relief when we come to painful states of mind and heart – such as loneliness, stress, suppressed anger or pressure to succeed – that are fuelled by a driving self. If seen with more authentic awareness, they are just habitual messages that come and go and the self that seems to power them cannot be found.

This is out of the box. A magical world opens, vast and flowing like a great river.

questions
that undo
the questioner

We are in an age of deconstruction, in which previously held dogmas and givens are taken to pieces and challenged. But the Wisdom mind would go further and deconstruct the one that deconstructs. Questions that have no real answer can take us right out of the construction business. In Zen practice, questions like 'what was your face before you were born?' are used to establish a destabilising state of uncertainty, which eventually exhausts the mind that is trying and failing to work it all out. Wisdom can then break through the exhausted conceptual mind like a flash of lightning. Similarly, if constantly maintained, questions like 'Who am I?' directly challenge the known and assumed reality, and gradually bring the realisation that we are not at all who we thought we were. We discover that the me is a repeating thought and assumption and that in truth we are made by life and are life, which is infinitely bigger than the little me. Then we have no choice but to let go into the world.

There are a multitude of ways and means, both Buddhist and non-Buddhist, of meeting the self, seeing its transparency and then seeing through it to merge with and join the vast world that subsequently opens. For example, some monks use visualisations of the death and decomposition of the body. Any meditation practice that expands the awareness of direct sensory raw material, rather than the processing of it – the sound of a bell, the sight of colour, light or a candle, the touch of the feet on the ground – will take us there. There are meditations and contemplations that remind us that we are made of the same elements as the rest of the universe and therefore part of it rather than a separate unit. Again and again in traditional texts the Buddha reminds listeners that they are nothing other than a load of digested porridge walking about. A very well-known practice is to deconstruct moments of experience, breaking them into their elements. A simple experience such as answering a question will have emotional, conceptual, sensory, physical, memory and consciousness aspects, as well as a sense of self as a background element. This is of course well-known in brain science, which knows how different brain areas and neural networks with different functions synchronise together to give the impression of one seamless experience. But as a practice it allows us to meet and become aware of all these elements, including a direct meeting with the 'ghost in the machine' as Gilbert Ryle's described Descartes's concept of mind-body dualism.'

All such practices take time and need to be gradual, as they face a fundamental fear: the self panics if there is a hint that it might disappear; it hangs on for dear life and resists any attempt to challenge its dominion. But sometimes there are situations that make us leap out of the self-story into a larger Wisdom perspective. Imagine if your doctor told you that you only had a month to live. What might happen? Suddenly everything might take on the most extraordinary importance and every moment could be precious and lived intensely. You might seize life and love, you might do things that you always longed to do but never dared, you might feel the depth and beauty of life. This is not just a visualisation, but the truth of things, as we never know how long we have and we can sense that life is rapidly slipping through our fingers. We can live like that. We can make this leap intentionally by dying a little in order to really live. 'die now into the now' is the instruction of the Advaita master Nisargadatta Maharaj.

can we be a wise fool?

The Wisdom mind does not keep to the same rules and conventions as the ordinary mind. It may get persecuted by others who feel threatened by it, or dismissed, or laughed at. In the story of the Emperor's New Clothes, the boy is lucky that the crowd didn't turn on him. Society desperately needs Wisdom, but is afraid of its iconoclastic power, which challenges commonly held beliefs. At worst, those with the Wisdom mind can be sent to mental hospitals. So sometimes we need to keep quiet or couch our Wisdom in the language of humour. From Jerry Seinfeld to Jennifer Saunders some of the greatest comedians of modern times permit the most painful truths to be openly expressed and laughed at. Forrest Gump, stepping on a pile of dog poo, led to the immortalisation of two words that summarise the human situation: 'shit happens!'.

A poignant symbol of humour as a vehicle for Wisdom is the Fool in the court of the king. In Shakespeare's tale of King Lear, the king (always an image of self and ego) gets carried away with himself. He demands proof of love from his daughters and respect, service, and obedience. The more he demands these things; the more life denies them to him. He loses his reason during a wild storm (the storm of life). The one voice that always tries to bring him back to sense and to pierce his ballooning ego is that of his Fool. For fear of losing his head, the Fool had to hide his Wisdom in cynical asides. 'He that has and a little tiny wit... Must make content with his fortunes fit / For the rain it raineth every day'. The Fool represents those thoughts and voices of Wisdom ('wit') that tell us to come back down to earth. In the spirit of the Beatles song, can we be 'the fool on the hill that sees the sun going down'?

Again and again we can experience the profound and liberating Wisdom that life is happening by itself

let go of the chains

The Greek philosopher Plato had a dramatic and rather terrifying parable of basic human ignorance. The parable portrays us all living in a cave. Outside the cave is a source of light that we cannot see. All we can see are shadows projected on the walls at the back of the cave, which we assume to be reality. We cannot turn to see the light outside the cave because we are fixed by chains. Only a few are now and then able to realise their true situation. Their hunger to know a deeper reality causes the chains to fall away, so they can turn to see the light shining from outside. In Plato's image, the light is the Wisdom of great and elevated insights. A Buddhist version would call the chains attachment and would see the light outside not only as great thoughts but as awakening to the selfless, changeable and free essence of all experiences.

This points to a profound truth that is hard for us to grasp. What we see and experience through the senses and perception and assume to be reality, are actually mental constructions that we built through learning, habits of conditioning, brain networks, assumptions, beliefs and consensus thinking. Conceptual consciousness keeps reaching out and constructing an apparently known world that is actually an illusion or dream. We do not realise that we are wearing the lenses of conditioning through which we

'Whatever we conceive it to be the reality is other than that'.

see everything. In Indian culture, this great illusion is called 'Maya'. It is not only inner explorers and spiritual practitioners that understand this. Insightful scientists and philosophers know that the reality that you perceive depends on the questions that you ask. This gets even more refined in quantum physics, which confirms that we cannot know the world as it is, since our observation is part of the reality and changes what is observed. This is an excellent definition of the Buddhist-inspired understanding of Wisdom.

It is very hard for us to accept that the world we know is illusory. However, once we see the shadows as shadows, the chains of attachment simply drop away. We can see the light once we allow the darkness. How do we see shadows as shadows? If we look closely at what arises in our perceptions and in our mind, if we look under the radar, we see that it is composed of a myriad of possibilities, most of them constructed by our memories and conditioning. They are appearances of themselves, but we cannot know or describe them independent of the lens through which we perceive them. As a famous Theravada Buddhist one-liner states: 'Whatever we conceive it to be the reality is other than that'.

Take the simple example of a tree. We assume that a tree that we see exists in the world as we see it. But we forget that every moment, every time we move our eyes and head, we are seeing it quite differently and certainly at it at different times it will look to us utterly different. It will look different to a child, a dog, an

Aborigine, to us if we have Alzheimer's or take a tiny amount of LSD, or if we see it with an awakened fresh view in which it appears new and original in every moment. The same is even truer of profound assumptions that rule our life and control much of our activity. For example, the assertion that 'I have a body, this body belongs to me, I am the owner of it', is a hugely powerful and obsessive assumption that, if examined carefully, cannot be true. It is a belief. Examination will tend to reveal the opposite: life is running the body and we are the spectator and live in it, but do not own it. All the cells of the body change every few years, but the sense of ownership does not. When we go to the toilet, do we cry that a bit of ourselves is being flushed down the pan? Clearly the body and the sense of ownership are separate from each other.

attachment to our views

Our identification with our views, opinions and thoughts and the conviction that they are true facts, is, according to Buddhist teachings, one of the four great attachments that are the source of suffering (the others are attachment to sensory experiences, to habits and rituals and the way things ought to be and to a belief in the existence of a self). We may tend to believe our views as right, and others' views as wrong, but this contracted place is asking for trouble. The Wisdom mind would always acknowledge that a thought, notion, or view is just a view. If someone comes at us with radically opposing and strong opinions, we can certainly offer our own view, but if we don't hold on tight to our rightness, then the challenge will never hurt us. Life will offer challenges, invasions and disturbances, but if we learn to be less identified and attached, we can receive all the challenges but stay steady, light and free in the midst of things.

A powerful example of the way attachments can cause us all a great deal of pain concerns the labelling of others. Black, Caucasian, Muslim, Jew, Liberal, Conservative – such labels cut down unique, precious and unfathomable human beings into a cipher. We need to question and let go of such unexamined views, social convictions and childhood conditioning.

Over many years we used to bring groups of Israelis and Palestinians together for peace-making workshops. The core element was an hour of deep listening in dyads in which Israelis and Palestinians told the stories of the struggles and challenges of their daily life and that of their families. In that hour a radical shift happened as the labels of 'them' and 'us' 'terrorist', 'occupier' and 'enemy' that sustain the intractable conflict were no longer relevant. In their place was a human being with pain behind the eyes and a personal world of heart, relationships and struggle. The change was irreversible – once the image is dropped and the view expands, one cannot go back to that limited place.

dancing with change

Wisdom doesn't hold on. It is not burdened with the past or stuck in imagined futures and imprisoned by expectations and comparisons. It allows us to be flexible, adaptable and to dance with the winds of change. It can be a bad day. We may be stuck in traffic on the motorway and everything looks dirty, drab, industrial, ugly, unfriendly. And we are impatient and late. But one instant is all it takes to utterly shift the view. We can be like the GPS navigation; if we go down the wrong road it gives an immediate blip and says 'Recalculating' or 'Rerouting'. All it takes inside us is the fluidity to be able to do an instant blip and go down another route. If our mind is flexible, we can feel the beauty of this same world, compassion for all the other folk stuck with us in their cars, and gratitude for the gift of this life itself.

coping with conflict

It may be difficult to understand how we can solve a problem without our usual strategies of weighing up the options and thinking about the best solution. Surely, we need the planning mind that explores options in order to make choices in life? Of course, much functional thinking is needed to act effectively in life. A simple thought that says, 'we've run out of milk, I will go and get some', is the right thought at the right time. But so much of our mental activity is about churning possibilities, imagining future scenarios and getting stuck in loops of: 'if... then'. It often leads to agitation, inaction and uncertainty and fails to deliver clarity and decisiveness. Wisdom can cut through the scripts and rapidly reveal answers to problems and dilemmas that are giving us trouble. It does so because we know ourselves more deeply, are more awake to the causes and conditions that brought us to this junction, are intimate with the world and have a better sense of what is right for us. It is the result of living with the powers of Mindfulness, with Trust expressed as our intimacy with, and availability for, whatever arises, with Energy to hone our actions, all maturing into the Wisdom of knowing what to do. We make choices and determine directions by a sense of immediate and intuitive insight, like a flash of lightning. Answers seem to come from beyond, are not entirely in our control and are more likely to arrive when watching the sea or the stars rather than sitting for hours in the office. Wisdom is less technical and less functional, but it recruits the Energy of a bigger, more creative and more expanded awareness.

Non-wisdom or ignorance is the way we sleepwalk into trouble. And conflict, one of the clearest examples of painful and intractable downstream, results from a lack of Wisdom. Conflict happens fast and easily, erupting at any moment between ourselves and partners, close family members, work colleagues, neighbours or groups we oppose. So how can we apply Wisdom to such situations? We would use Mindfulness and Calm to create a sacred pause in the rapid and automatic reactivity. We can ground ourselves in our body and belly. This will allow us to expose the scripts and processes and see what is really happening: the words of the other, our buttons being pressed, the anger rising, the pressure to respond and defend oneself – the whole chain begins to unravel. We can also see and come down off the tree of justifications, interpretations and beliefs. As we keep meeting conflict in this way, we will increasingly see how it all passes by and leaves us peaceful and present. Wisdom follows Mindfulness as it reveals the big picture and this can take the pain out of such challenging situations. In particular, we can see behind the eyes of the other as a human being with needs just like ourselves. They may be expressing their own fears and insecurities. As we put ourselves in the shoes of the other, we can see both of us caught up in conditions and our heart can open.

There is a Tibetan story of two friends who are walking in the marketplace. Suddenly one of them gets hit by a stick. He immediately starts shouting at the stick. His friend asks: 'don't you think it is more sensible to shout at the hand holding the stick and not the stick?' 'Of course,' he replied, and began shouting at the hand. His friend then said that it would perhaps be more sensible to shout at the person whose hand was wielding the stick. The man then began shouting at the person. His friend now said: 'you don't know why this person hit you. Maybe he is really suffering, maybe he hasn't eaten for ages. You should shout at the conditions that actually made him hit you with the stick.' 'Yes, of course', the man agreed. Then he stopped.

See what is really happening: the words of the other, our buttons being pressed, the anger rising, the pressure to respond and defend oneself – the whole chain begins to unravel.

'I can't shout at conditions. Conditions are potentially endless And conflict, one of the clearest examples of painful and intractable downstream, results from a lack of Wisdom. the whole universe. I can't shout at the whole universe.' 'Exactly,' said his friend.

Once I was looking after two of my grandchildren, aged five and seven. They were playing when the older boy walked away and the five-year-old came to sit next to me. 'What happened?' I asked. 'We had an argument she answered. 'But you are so calm about it', I commented. 'Yes, because I know he will get over it in a few minutes, he just doesn't know it yet.' That is Wisdom.

making a difference

Wisdom is engaged with life, not hiding in some sacred closet. When we consider going out in the world and making change, we may often feel discouraged by issues that hold us back. We may feel that the task is beyond us, that we are helpless – just little me in a big hostile messy world – or that we are not ready. But Wisdom would challenge all these stories by showing them to be constructions that are beliefs rather than the truth of things. And when we no longer invest in such disempowering narratives,

our kind compassionate heart, our intentions to heal and reduce suffering in the world and our life of goodness and harmony will naturally emerge unhindered and we will find ourselves intending to make change and just going out and doing it.

Still, we may be faced with a tendency for measurement of success or failure and we may be held hostage to assessments of outcomes and expectations. Decades of peace work around the world often appear to have limited impact on the conflicts they seek to ease. Were they a waste of time? Did they fail? We are not in charge of karma, life does what it wants with our contributions. All we can do is offer ourselves and let go of measuring results.

The intention and hunger for a better world is not enough. If we look carefully, we will see that what does the job of making change in the world are the qualities we manifest, not the outcomes we want. The writing, speaking, acting or campaigning that moves hearts and minds can only happen because they are the manifestation of qualities and skills that are part of us. As we develop a Wisdom mind, our personality changes. It moves slowly and steadily away from the well-worn tracks of self-interest, busyness, identity, coping, success and failure, to the exploration and enjoyment of more refined qualities of being. Many of these qualities have been discussed already in this book. They include inquiry and reflection, authenticity, generosity as a way of life (dana), moral sensitivity, renunciation, patience, Calm and ease,

Energy, love, determination and equanimity. These qualities become the raw material of our thoughts, our daily experiences, our insights and our engagement with life.

As we pay for something in the supermarket, act ecologically, receive a gift or help another person or animal, it will not be mechanical and meaningless, but a manifestation of the deep truth that the world is made of nothing other than giving and receiving. As we walk past shops, we may experience the joy of renunciation, of being satisfied with less. As we speak, we may explore the ethics of our language: is it true, is it helpful, is it kind? These qualities become the objects of Mindfulness themselves. We will be aware of how the situations unfold, but at the same time watch how our qualities express themselves and modulate themselves through the experiences. Our doing in the world, indeed our whole life, becomes the joyful manifestation of refined qualities that we naturally offer out to everyone and everything. From that place, we can go out and make a difference in the world.

What happens if we keep going with the deep exploration of the nature of experience, expanding the boundaries of our consciousness and of the unknown, peeling off layers of conditioning, one by one, to reveal the ultimacy which they obscured? We will find that we gradually live with more and more pure awareness. And it has a taste of perfection, as there is nothing wrong in awareness itself, it is just awareness, like

space or the sky. And just as clouds can't disturb the sky, so if we rest more in the sky-like nature of pure awareness, objects and appearances will have less and less capacity to disturb. The singing of a bird can lift our heart, open our awareness and remind us that nothing is missing.

The world itself will look and feel quite different, more universal and more unitary, as awareness reveals the interconnectedness of things. It sees only contingency and has no need to chop everything into discrete and definable objects/pieces. Everything is made by

everything else. Linear causation is not the way the universe or life functions. 'Which came first, the chicken or the egg?' is a problem for the ordinary perception. But for the Wisdom mind the only problem is the question itself, which shows our need to understand what causes what and what comes next, so as to feel safer. One could say that the eye is needed in order to see light, but surely light elicited eyes in living beings. I have a vegetable garden and grow vegetables for food. But what is really happening? The vegetables sustain me, I sustain them, and the earth sustains us both. We are a nutritive, interdependent cycle and I am as much part of the ecology as every radish.

A bigger view of things also radically changes our search for meaning. Faced with the great unknown, we ask: 'What is the meaning of life?' The question is crucial, fuelling our search and driving our inner journey of discovery, although it is unable to provide more than provisional and unsatisfying answers. The Wisdom mind is no longer interested in questions about the meaning of life, which imply a life separate from the questioner. Instead, the question itself transforms into amazement. We become interested in meaningfulness, not meaning, and know that every moment of life cannot be other than constantly and entirely meaningful.

...and to enlightenment

Wisdom works, clearing the ground for a constantly expanded view. The usual constructions of the mind become less and less relevant and we find ourselves at one with what arises, with less need for description, construction, definition, or interpretation. In the Buddha's poetic description, he likened this Awakening or Enlightenment to breaking the beams of a house. The house is the structure of the mind, the habitual building of the world. It is made of attachment and once he could let go of all clinging, whether to needs, to the self, or to the known defined world, the whole house collapsed. 'You shall build no more. Your rafters are dislodged and the ridgepole is broken. All craving is ended; My heart is as one with the unmade.' Awakening allowed him to break the spell, smash the house and rest in Being, in the unmade and the unconstructed or the Unconditioned, as it is often called in Buddhist terms. We can sense it as the possibility of wide-open spaces instead of constructions, unimaginable freedom in which all moments are unbounded and timeless.

This is not an all-or-nothing heroic mission in which we are either imprisoned in Plato's Cave or totally free. The process is gradual and continuous and bears fruit all along the way. For the journey is more important than the destination. We keep

294 | The Five Powers

deconstructing bits of the structure, opening windows, seeing more gaps through the walls of the self and world and as we do, so we find ourselves experiencing greater and greater intimacy and that is the reward. Our heart finds interconnection with the world, which always welcomes us with wide open arms. We absorb the tweets of love from the sky and the moon and the small birds under the bushes and send back our own.

gone beyond

As we have seen, the Wisdom mind always takes us to a more universal and less personal sphere. Awakening cannot be owned by anyone. Once the Buddha was asked: 'How do you recognise an Enlightened person?' He answered: 'You recognise them because you can't find them.' The questioner was flummoxed by this answer and asked the Buddha to explain what he meant: 'has the man disappeared, does he simply not exist or is he in some perpetual state of well-being?' This is what the Buddha answered: 'When a person has gone beyond, then there is nothing by which you can measure him. Anything that can be said about him is no longer relevant; but you cannot say that he does not exist.'

This all points to the culmination of the Wisdom mind as 'Gone Beyond' categories or definitions describable by language. The Buddha described himself by the unfathomable word Tathagata, meaning something like 'Gone to Being'. The normal mind cannot grasp and hang on to such states, just as the baby cannot conceive of the womb that bore it. Our normal mind needs to let go of itself and drop into its source, like a wave returning to the ocean. And then we will discover that Wisdom was part of us from the very beginning. Wisdom savors every moment in the present, as we move forward into endless possibility and opportunity.

References

Trust

Mondalek, A., Quote from Don Pepper in: *Instant MBA: A Culture of Trust Is Directly Connected to Productivity Levels*. Business Insider, 28/6/2013.

Eliot, T.S., *The Four Quartets*. London: Faber & Faber (2001).

Mindfulness

Rapgay, L., & Bystrisky, A., Classical mindfulness: An introduction to its theory and practice for clinical application. *Annals of the New York Academy of Sciences*, 1172: 148-62 (2009).

Brown, K. W., Ryan, R. M., & Creswell, J. D., Mindfulness: Theoretical foundations and evidence for its salutary effects. *Psychological Inquiry*, 18: 211-237 (2007).

Pascoe MC, et al., Mindfulness mediates the physiological markers of stress: Systematic review and meta-analysis. *J Psychiatr Res.*, 95:156-178 (2017).

Sutcliffe K.M. et al., Mindfulness in Organisations: A Cross Level Review. *Annu. Rev. Organ. Psychol. Organ. Behav.*, 3:55–81 (2016).

Shahidi S, et al., Effectiveness of mindfulness-based stress reduction on emotion regulation and test anxiety in female high school students. *J Educ Health Promot.*, 4:87 (2017).

Hofmann SG, Gómez AF., Mindfulness-based interventions for anxiety and depression. *Psychiatr Clin North Am*, 40:739-749 (2017).

Biegel, G. M., et al., Mindfulness-based stress reduction for the treatment of adolescent psychiatric outpatients: A randomized clinical trial. *Journal of Consulting and Clinical Psychology*, 77: 855–866 (2009).

Chiesa, A. and Serretti, A., Mindfulness-based interventions for chronic pain: a systematic review of the evidence. *J. Alternative and Complementary Medicine,* 17:83-93 (2011).

Garland SN, et al., The quest for mindful sleep: a critical synthesis of the impact of mindfulness-based interventions for insomnia. *Curr Sleep Med Rep.,* 2(3):142-151 (2016).

Zhang J, et al., Effects of mindfulness-based therapy for patients with breast cancer: A systematic review and meta-analysis. *Complement Ther Med.,* 26:1-10 (2016).

Haller H, et al., Mindfulness-based interventions for women with breast cancer: an updated systematic review and meta-analysis. *Acta Oncol.,* 56(12):1665-1676 (2017).

The Foundations of Mindfulness Discourse (Satipatthana Sutta). Thanissaro Bhikkhu (Tr.) Majjhima Nikaya, MN 10.

Hamlet, Act 2, Scene 2.

Zaiderman, Y. et.al., self-specific processing in the meditating brain: a MEG neurophenomenology study. *Neuroscience of Consciousness,* 1–13 (2016).

Hamlet, Act 2, Scene 2.

Energy

Byrne, A. & Byrne, D.G., The effect of exercise on depression, anxiety and other mood states: a review, *Journal of Psychosomatic Research,* 37: 565-574 (1993).

Brainard, J. et al., Health implications of disrupted circadian rhythms and the potential for daylight as therapy. *Anesthesiology*, 122: 1170-1175 (2015).
Wordsworth, William. *Tintern Abbey*.

Maha-Saccaka Sutta, Thanissaro Bhikkhu (Tr.) Majjhima Nikaya 36.

Bhikkhu Bodhi ed. Anguttara Nikaya: *Book of Fours* II93 verse 3 p. 474.

Devadaha Sutta. Thanissaro Bhikkhu (Tr.) Majjhima Nikaya 101.

Eliot, T.S. *The Four Quartets*, London: Faber & Faber. (2001).

Calm

Sample, I., Shocking but true: students prefer jolt of pain to being made to sit and think. *The Guardian*, 3/7/2014.

Pablo Neruda, *Keeping Quiet*.

Pablo Neruda, Extravagaria, (Tr.) Alastair Reid, Noonday Press; Bilingual edition (2001).
Macbeth Act 5, Scene 5.

Rumi. *The Essential Rumi*. (tr. Coleman Barks), HarperOne, (2004).

Eliot, T.S. *The Four Quartets* Faber, (2001).

Wisdom

Wordsworth, W. *Tintern Abbey*.

Resources

The Five Powers online course

Stephen Fulder teaches an online course on The Five Powers.
The course extends knowledge and practice in developing and using
The Five Powers in our daily life. It is composed of eight video talks,
eight audio guided meditations, written materials, exercises and the
possibility to communicate with the teacher.
Go to www.stephenfulder.com

Further reading

Stephen Fulder. *What's Beyond Mindfulness: Waking Up To This Precious Life.*
Watkins, (2019).

Tara Brach. *Radical Acceptance: Embracing Your Life with the Heart of a
Buddha.* Bantam, (2004).

Thich Nhat Hanh. *Peace in Every Step: The Path of Mindfulness in Everyday
Life.* Bantam, (1992).

Jack Kornfield. *The Wise Heart: A Guide to the Universal Teachings of
Buddhist Psychology.* Penguin/Random House, (2009).

Rob Burbea. *The Seeing That Frees: Meditations on Emptiness and Dependent
Arising* Hermes Amara, (2015).

John Welwood. *Towards a Psychology of Awakening.* Shambhala, (2002).

Christopher Titmuss. *Light on Enlightenment: Revolutionary Teachings on the
Inner Life.* Rider, (1998).

Donald Rothberg. *The Engaged Spiritual Life: A Buddhist Approach to Transforming Ourselves and the World.* Beacon Press, (2006).

Jack Kornfield. *A Path with Heart: A Guide Through the Perils and Promises of Spiritual Life.* Bantam, (1993).

Acknowledgements

It's been a long road, one that took
Trust, Faith, Energy, creativity and knowledge.

Stephen Fulder, Alessandro Sanna, Rohan Saxena,
Tamar Bar-Dayan, Rebecca Citrin, Rachel Mills, Kate Adams
– each had it all.

Thank you for being such a great team and helping to bring
my idea and vision, the culmination of two years' work,
into such a life-changing book.

Daniella De-Nur